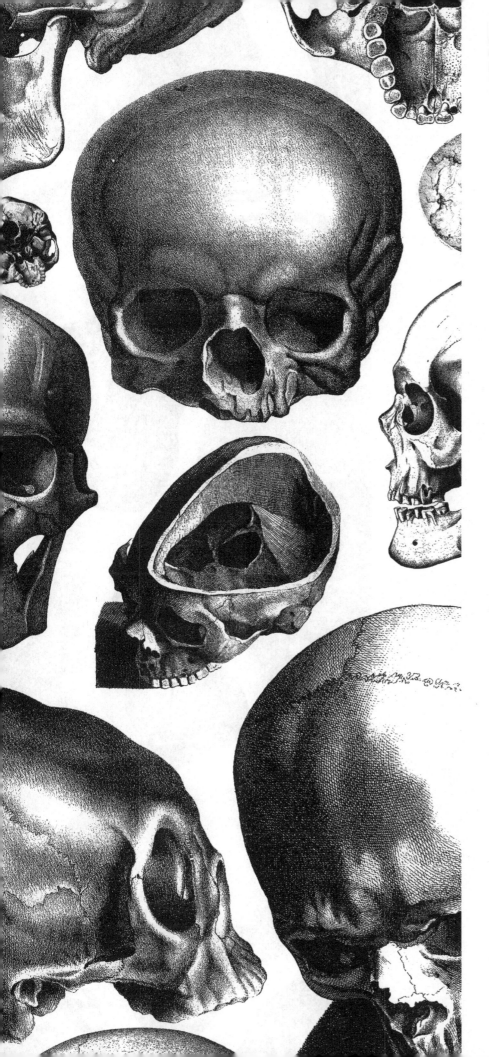

MW00804520

NUMBER ONE

SKULLS & SKELETONS

AN IMAGE ARCHIVE FOR
ARTISTS *And* DESIGNERS

EDITIONS
Vault

INTRODUCTION

Skulls & Skeletons, An Image Archive and Drawing Reference Book for Artists and Designers is a collection of 173 high-resolution, digitised 17th and 18th-century anatomical drawings for use in personal, or commercial creative projects. Whether you are looking for a comprehensive collection of anatomical images of the human skeleton to use as a reference for illustration, or a stunning collection of rare artistic anatomical artwork for use in graphics projects or digital collages, this book has got you covered.

Image Download Included:

We have carefully restored the artwork and provided a download link within the publication where you will locate high-resolution files in JPEG format to speed up your workflow. No scanning necessary! Follow the instructions found within the book and gain instant access to all images featured.

We hope you enjoy this resource.

VAULT EDITIONS

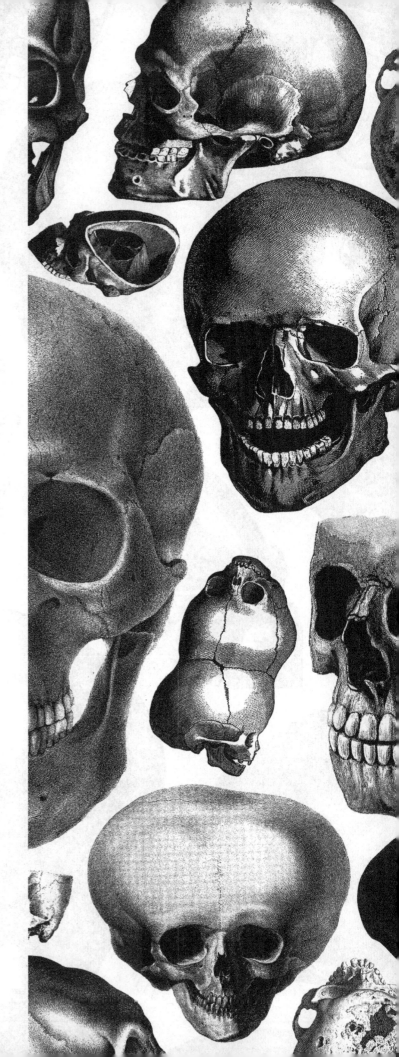

TABLE OF CONTENTS

DOWNLOAD YOUR FILES

Downloading your files is simple. To access your digital files, please go to the last page of this book and follow the instructions.

For technical assistance, please email:
info@vaulteditions.com

Bibliographical Note

This book is a new work created by Vault Editions Ltd.

ISBN: 978-1-925968-44-6

SKULLS & SKELETONS

VAULT EDITIONS

XXXIII

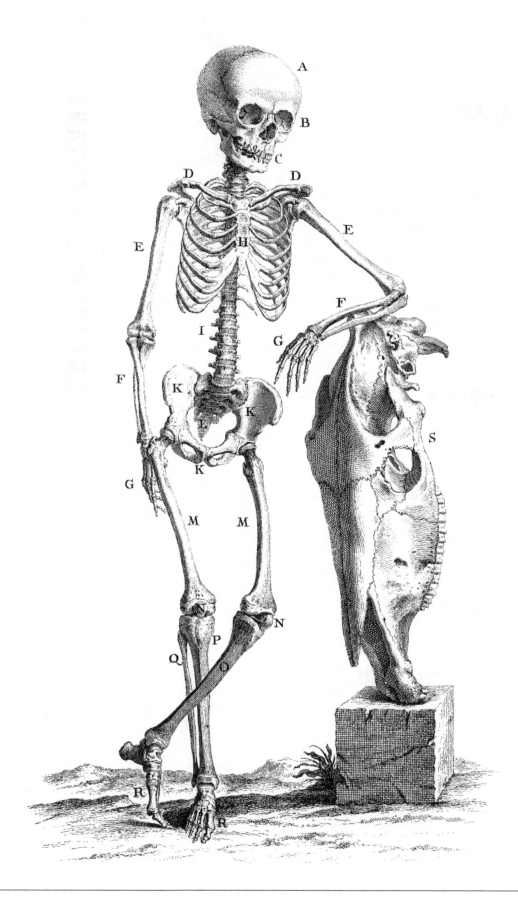

XXXVI

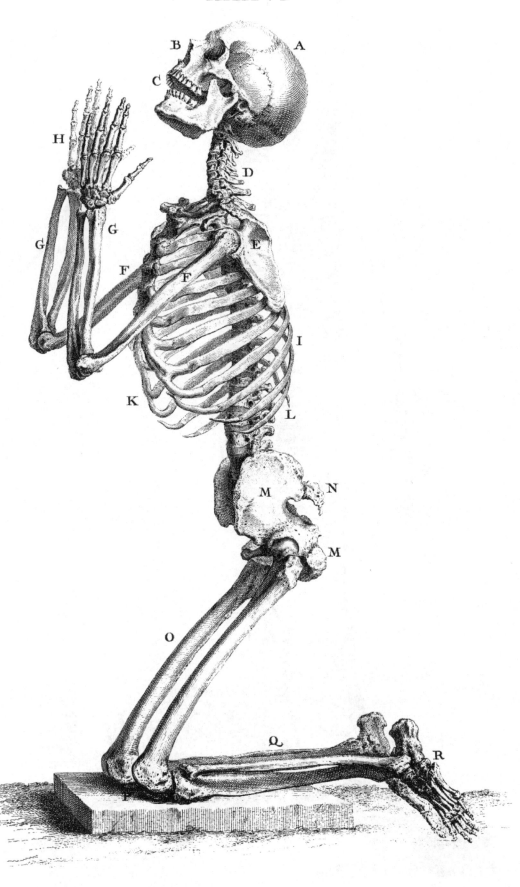

XXXII

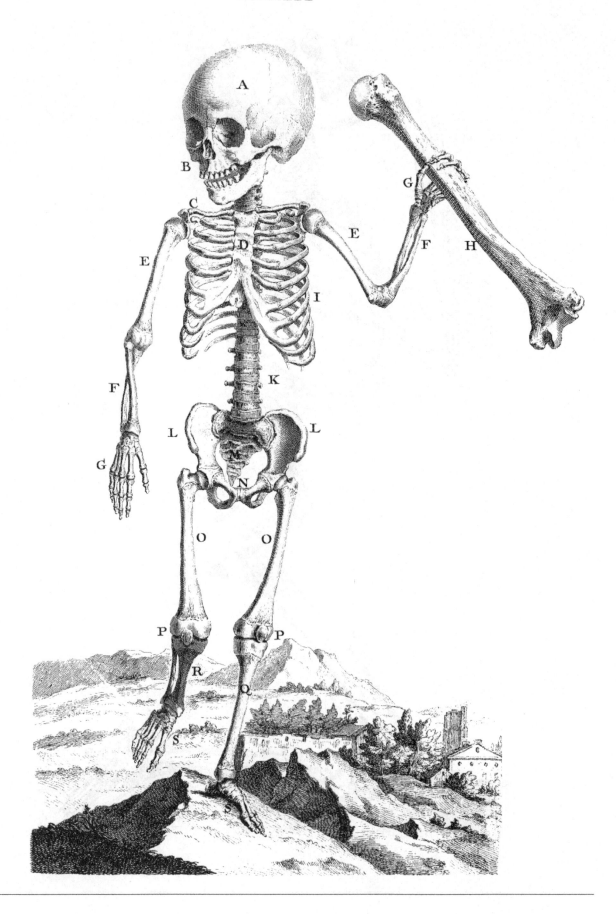

XXXVII

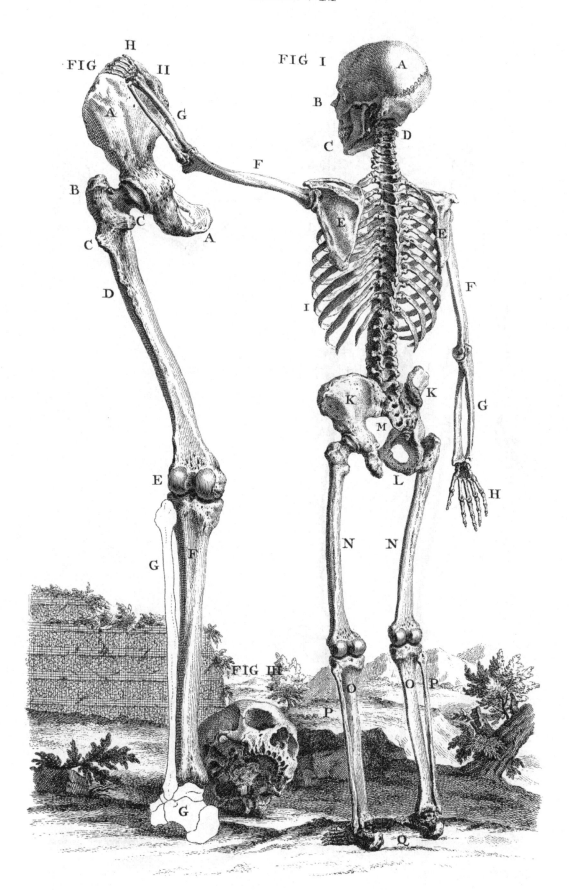

SKULLS AND SKELETONS

XXXV

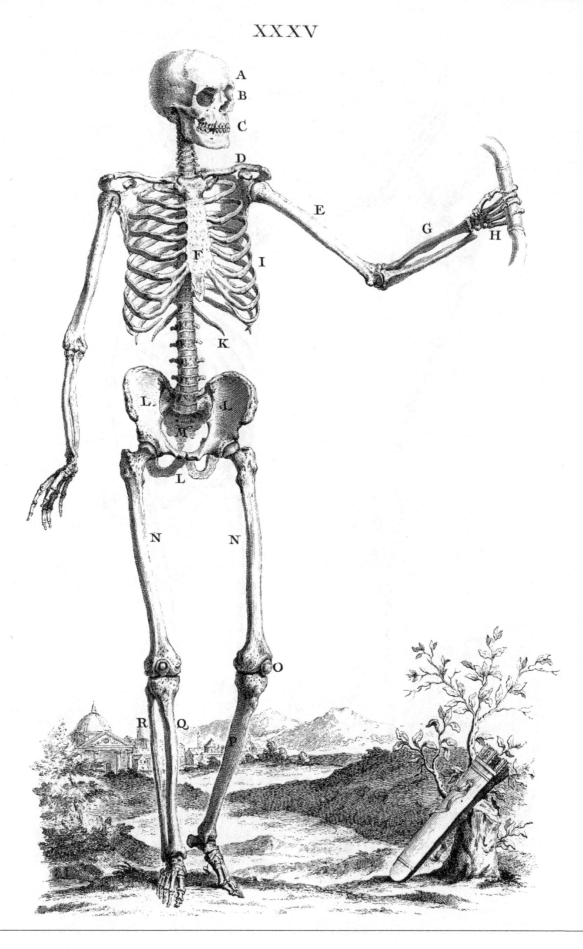

XXXIV

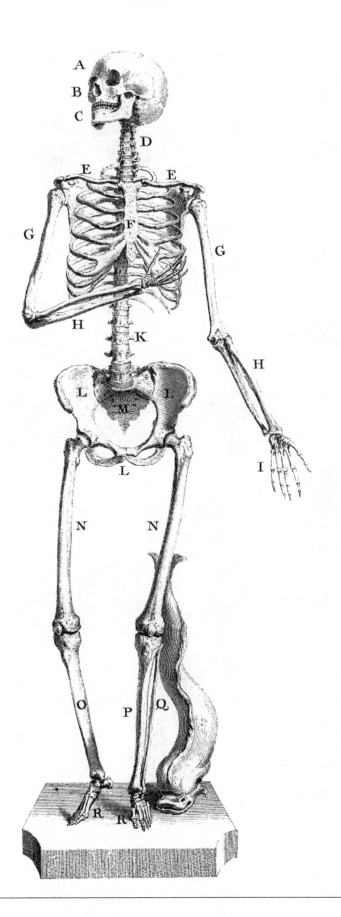

SKULLS AND SKELETONS

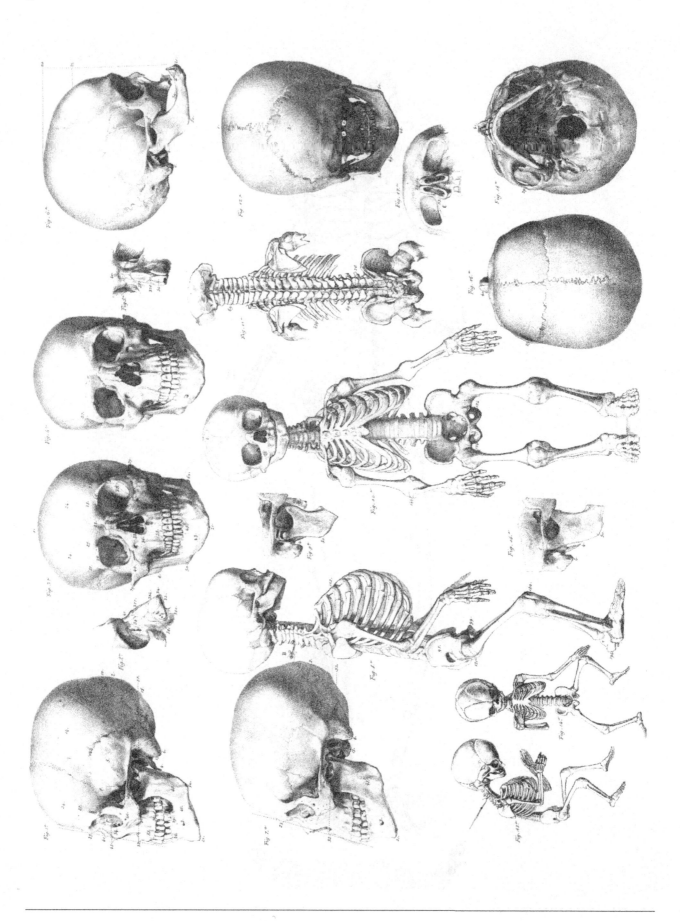

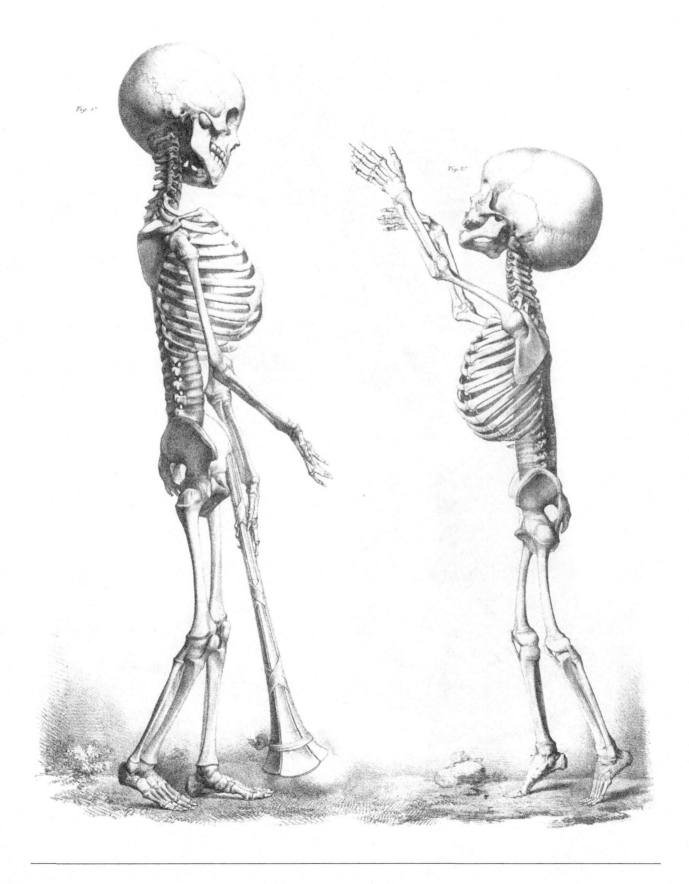

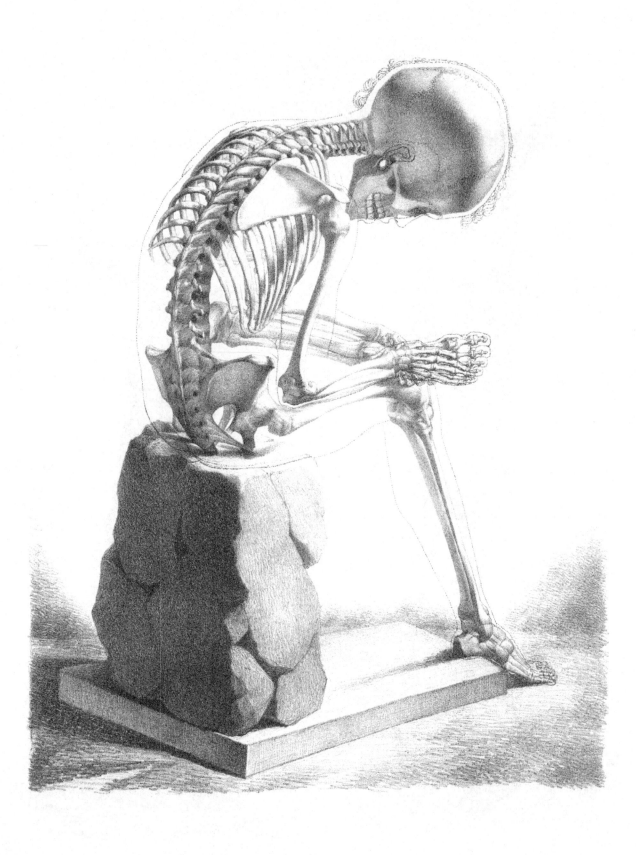

SKULLS AND SKELETONS

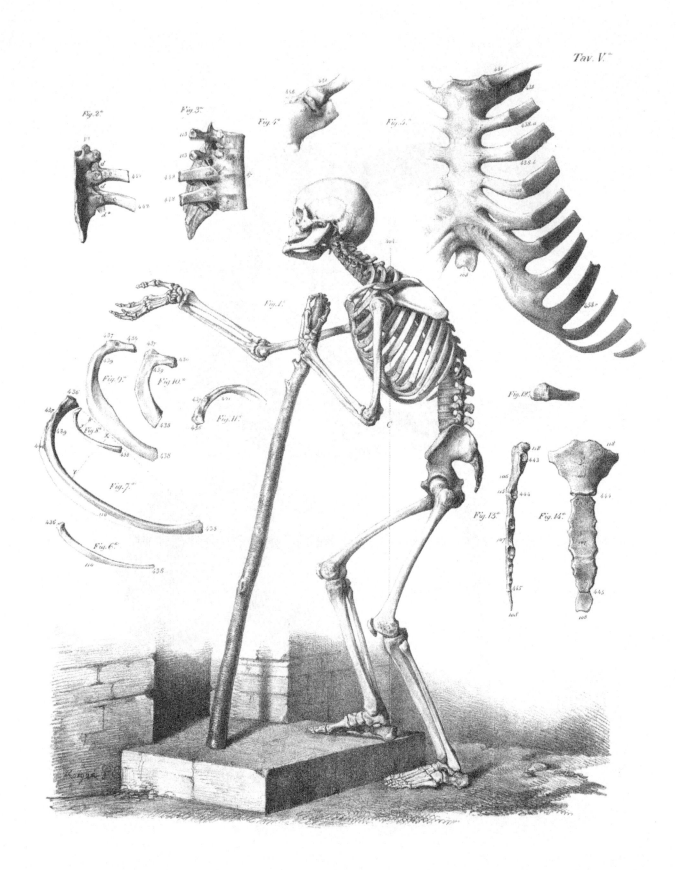

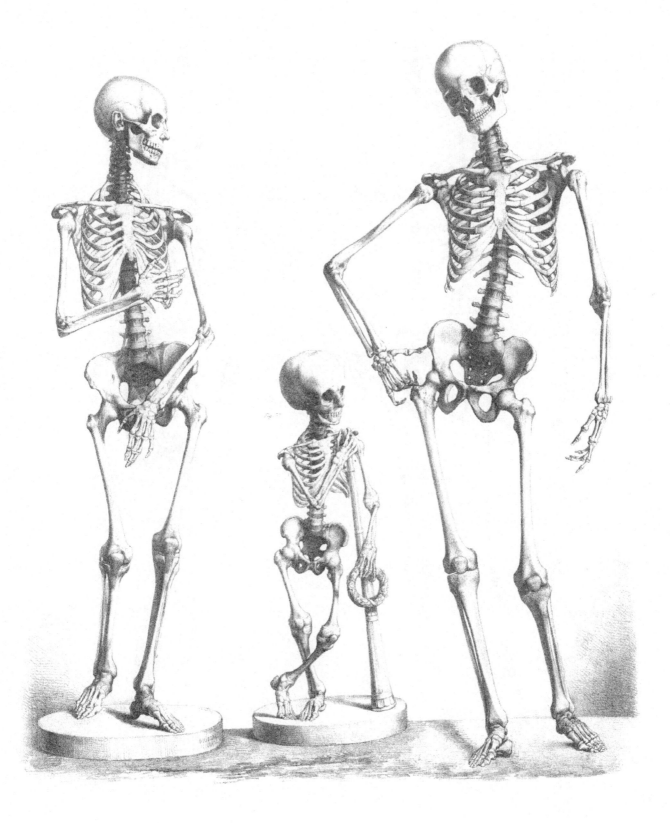

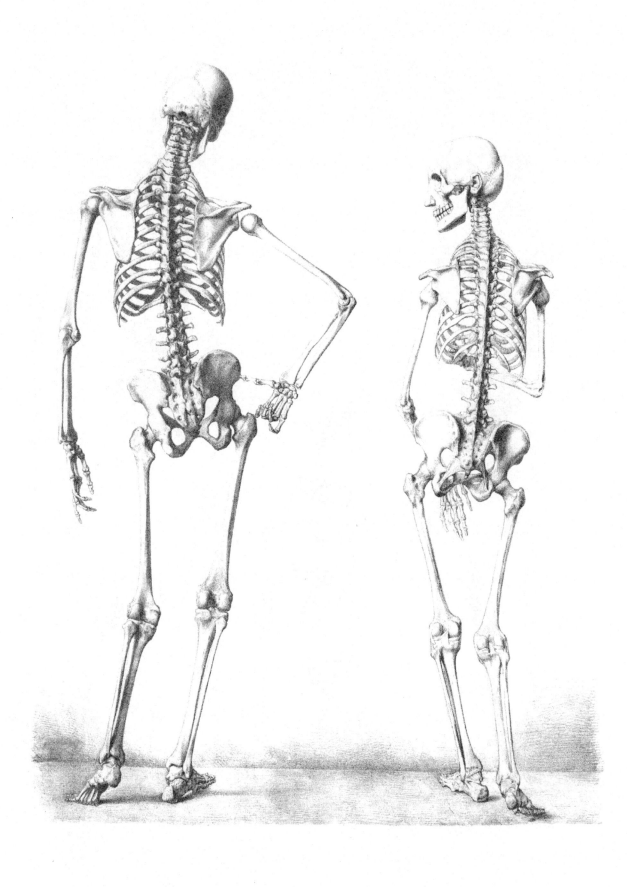

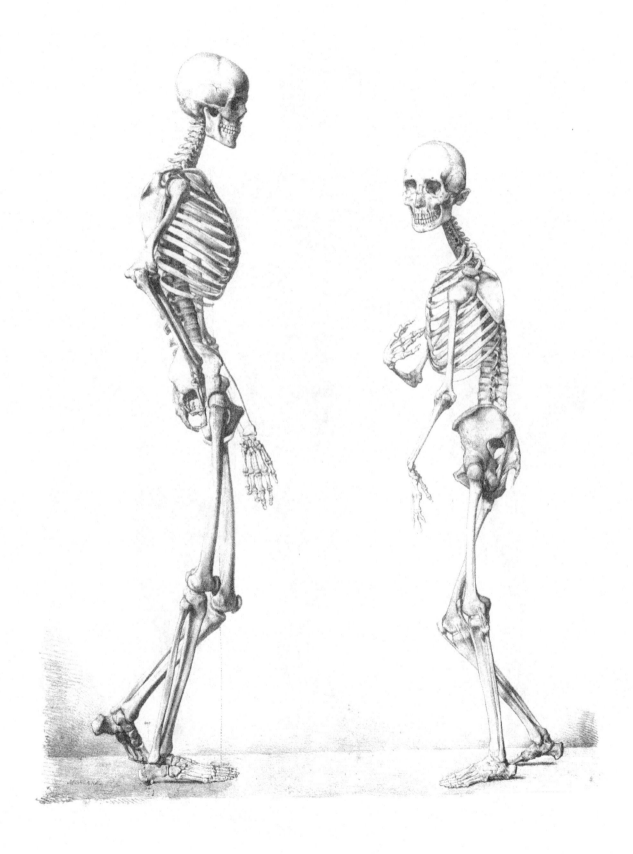

PLATE II.

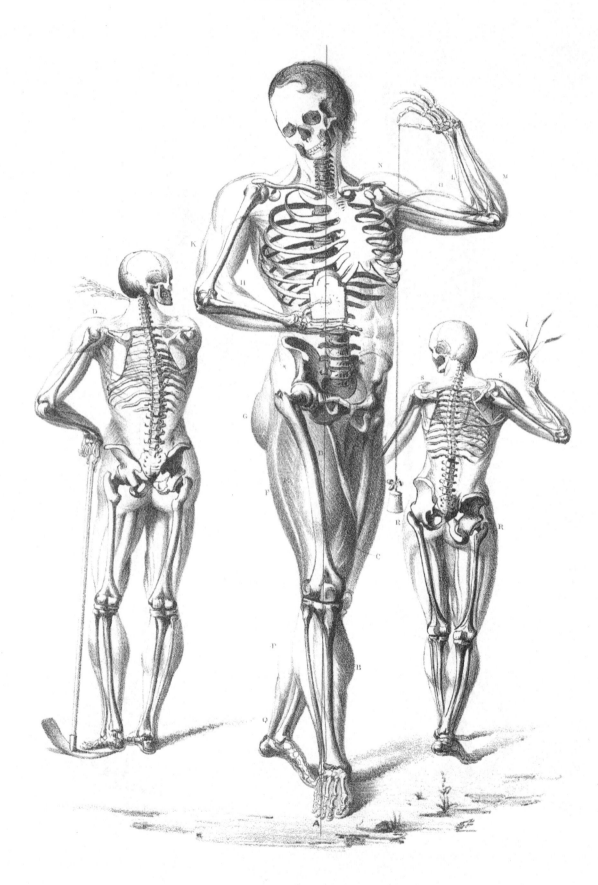

PLATE III.

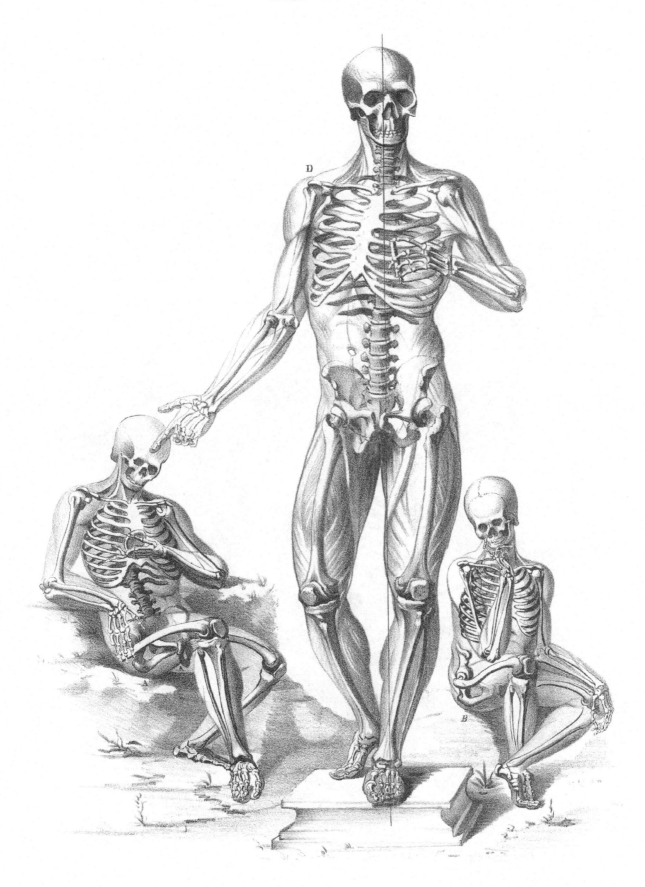

PLATE IV.

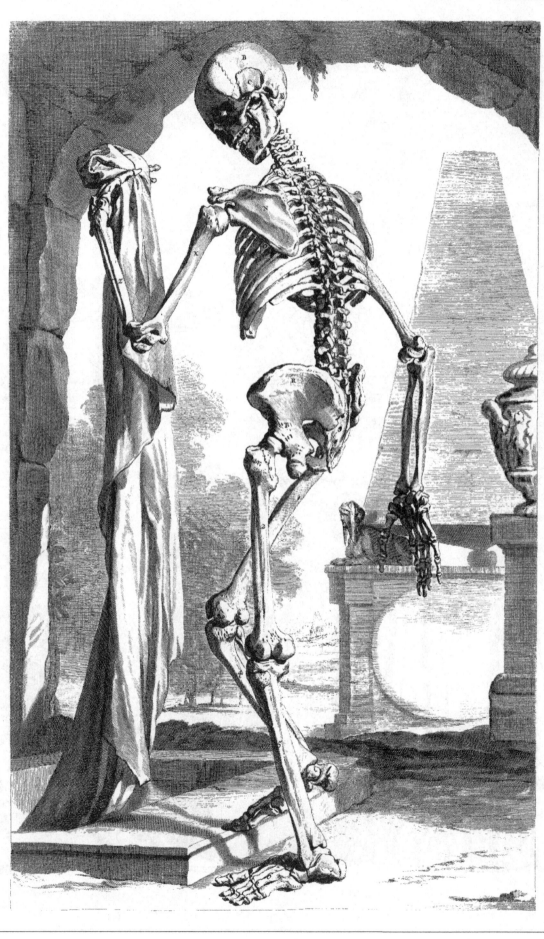

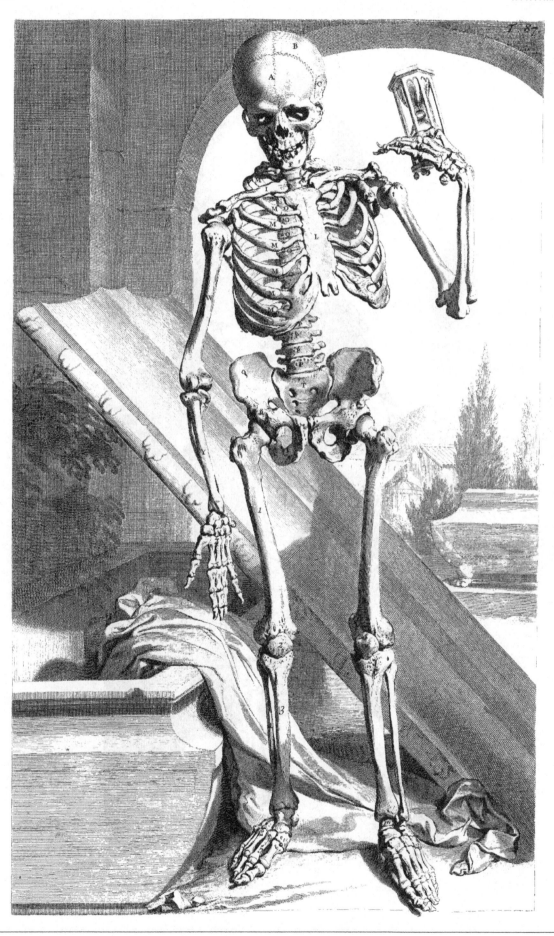

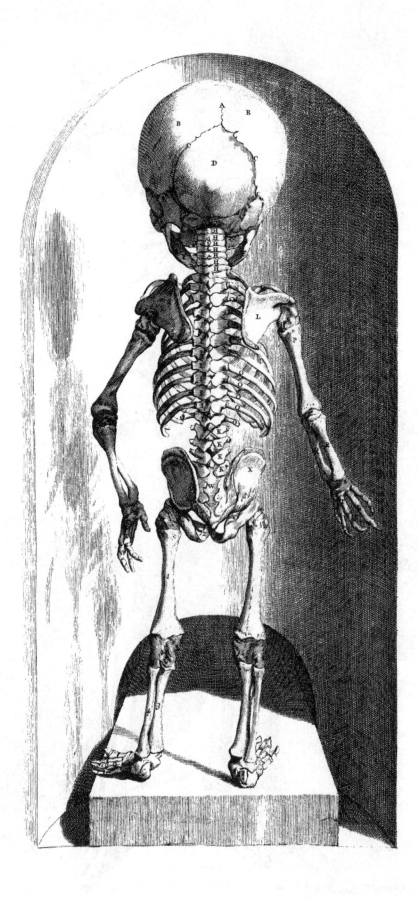

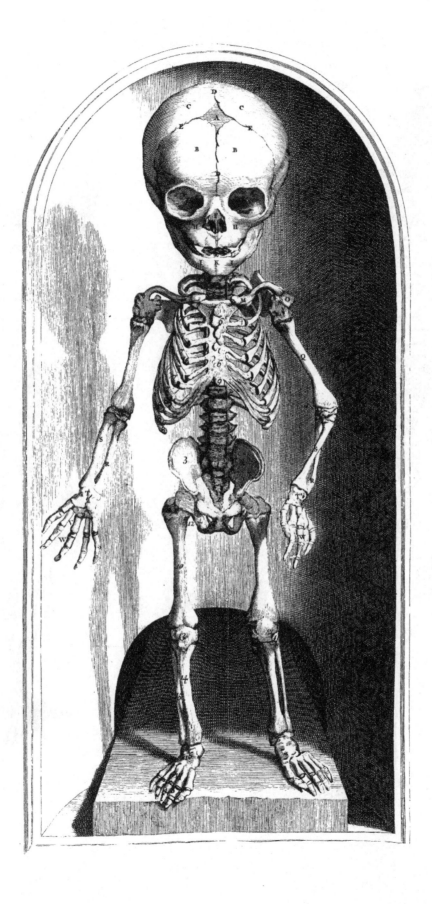

SKULLS AND SKELETONS

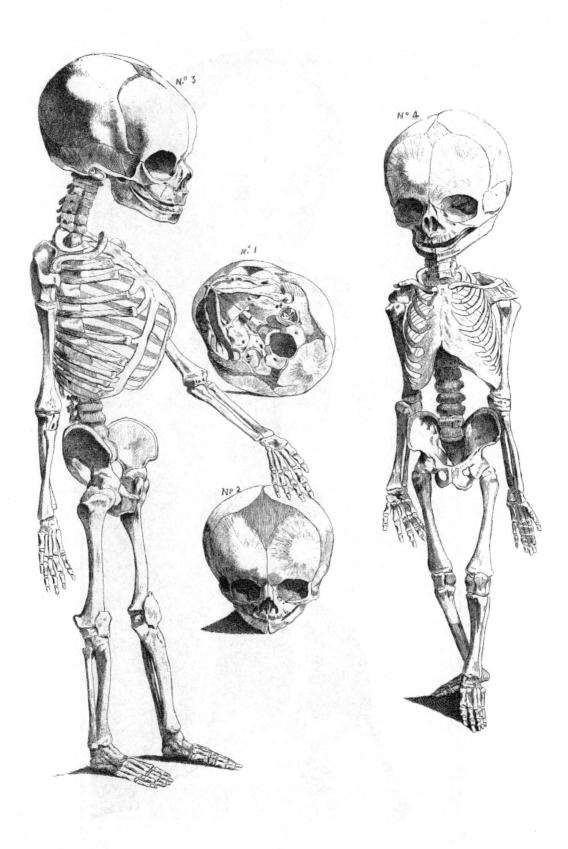

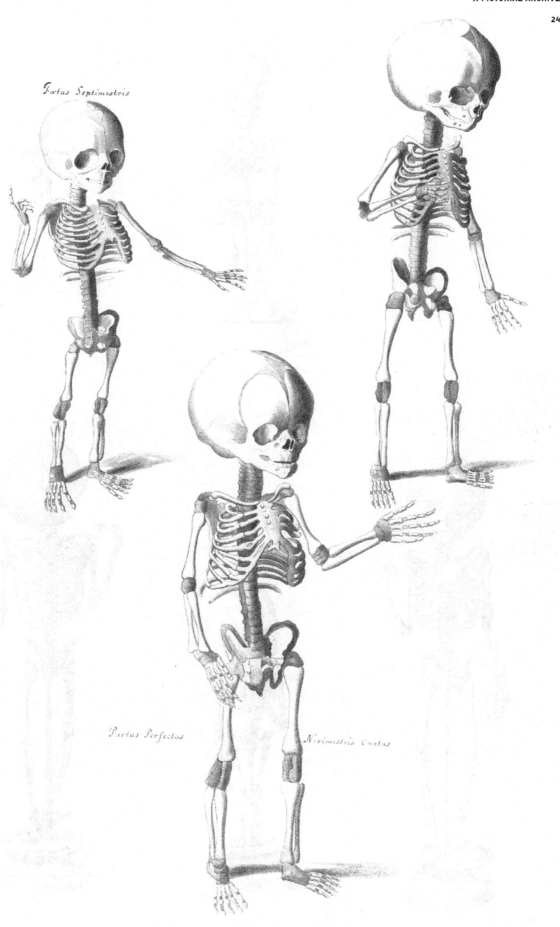

Fœtus Septimestris

Partus Perfectus *Novimestris Unatus*

SKULLS AND SKELETONS

Fig. 1.

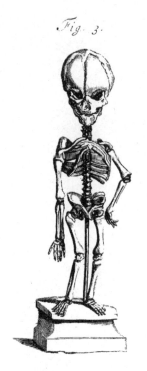

Fig. 3.

Fig. 2.

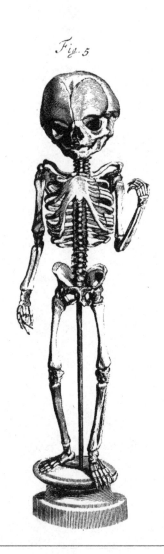

Fig. 5.

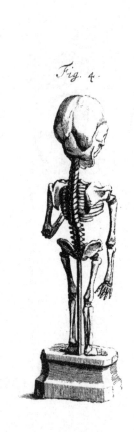

Fig. 4.

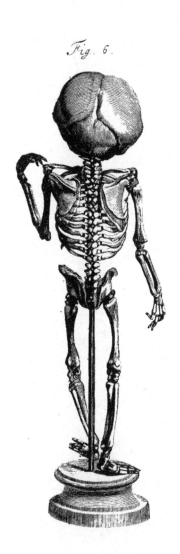

Fig. 6.

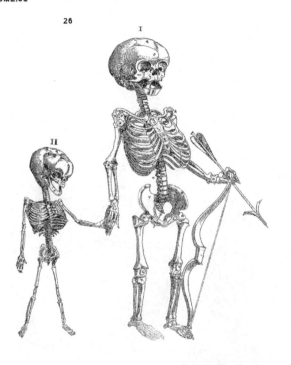

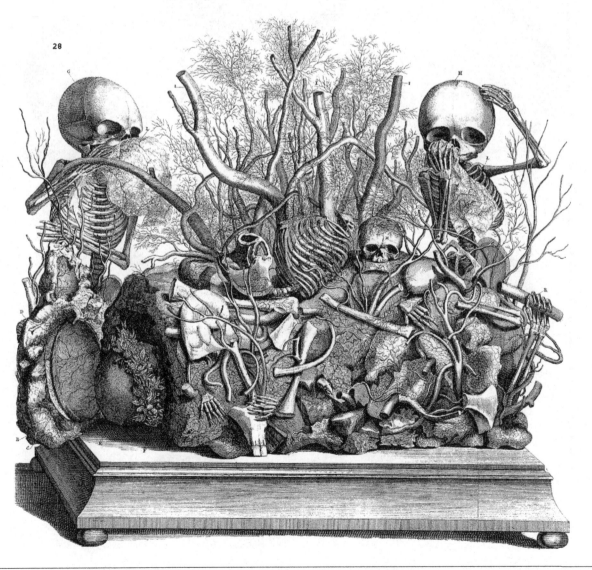

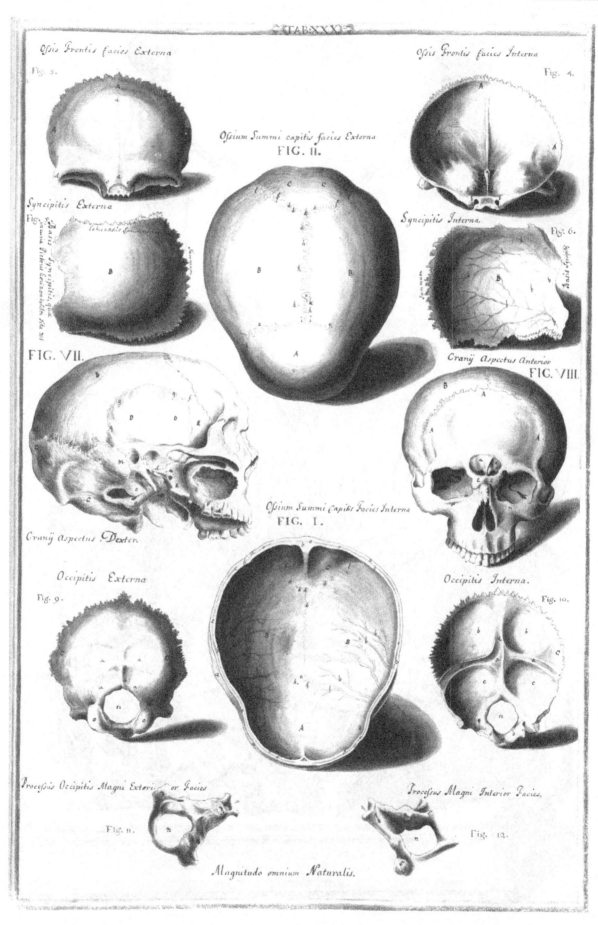

TAB.XXXV.

Ossis Frontis facies Externa

Fig. 3.

Ossis Frontis facies Interna

Fig. 4.

Ossium Summi capitis facies Externa
FIG. II.

Syncipitis Externa

Fig.

Syncipitis Interna.

Fig. 6.

FIG. VII.

Cranÿ Aspectus Anterior
FIG. VIII.

Cranÿ Aspectus Dexter.

Ossium Summi Capitis facies Interna
FIG. I.

Occipitis Externa

Fig. 9.

Occipitis Interna.

Fig. 10.

Processus Occipitis Magni Exterior Facies

Fig. 11.

Processus Magni Interior Facies,

Fig. 12.

Magnitudo omnium Naturalis.

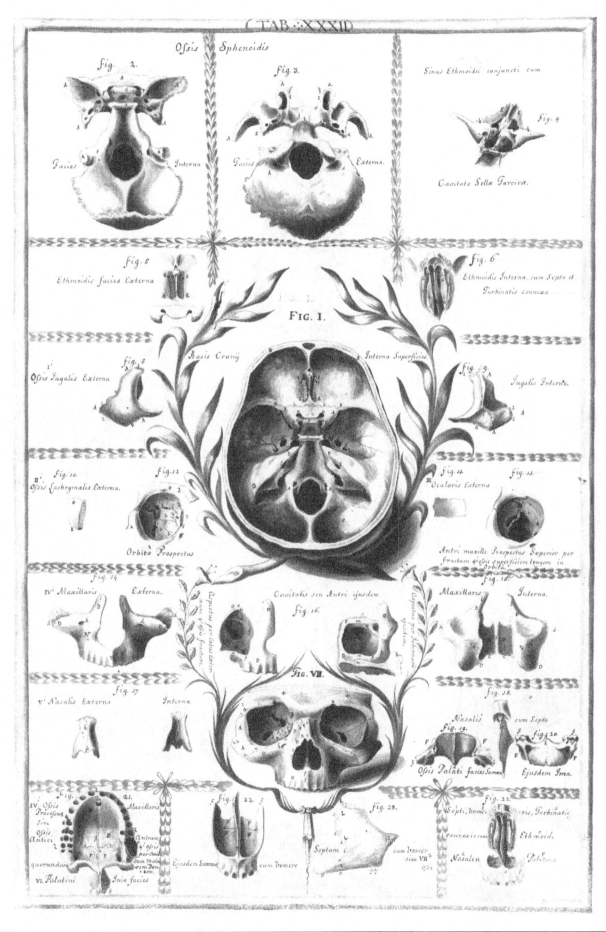

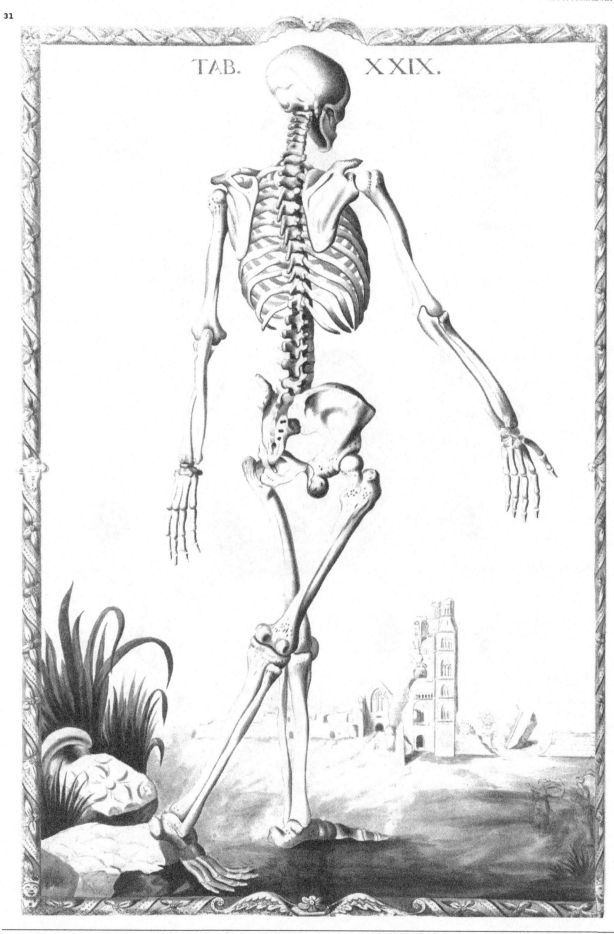

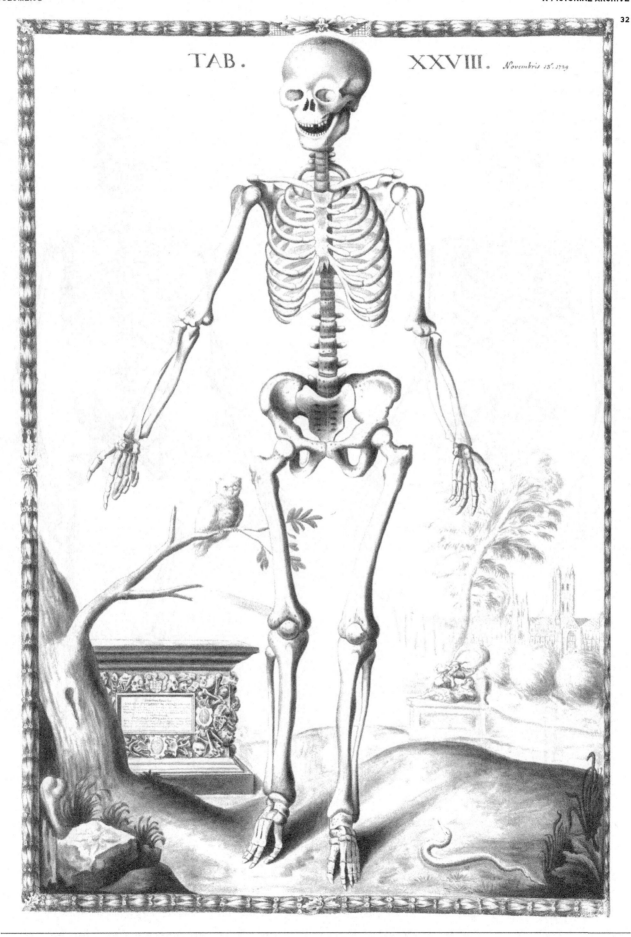

TAB. XXVIII. *Novembris 18. 1729*

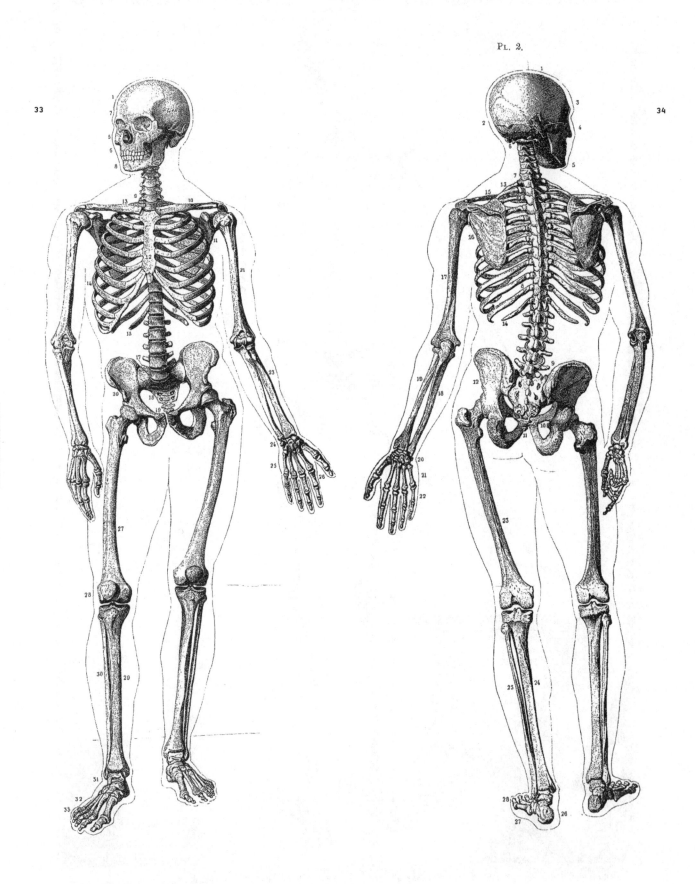

PL. 2.

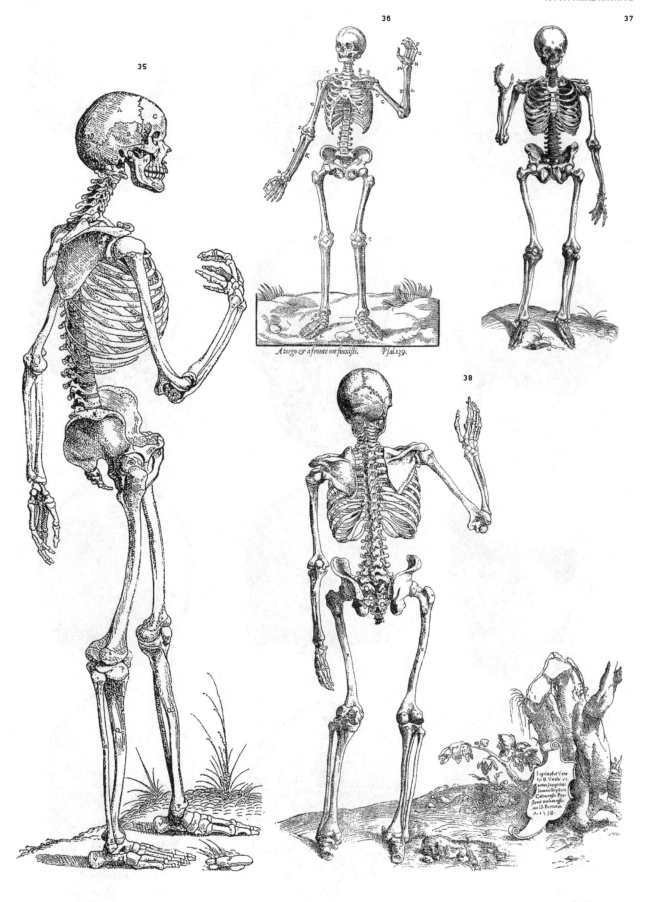

35

36

37

A tergo & a fronte me finxisti.   Psal.139.

38

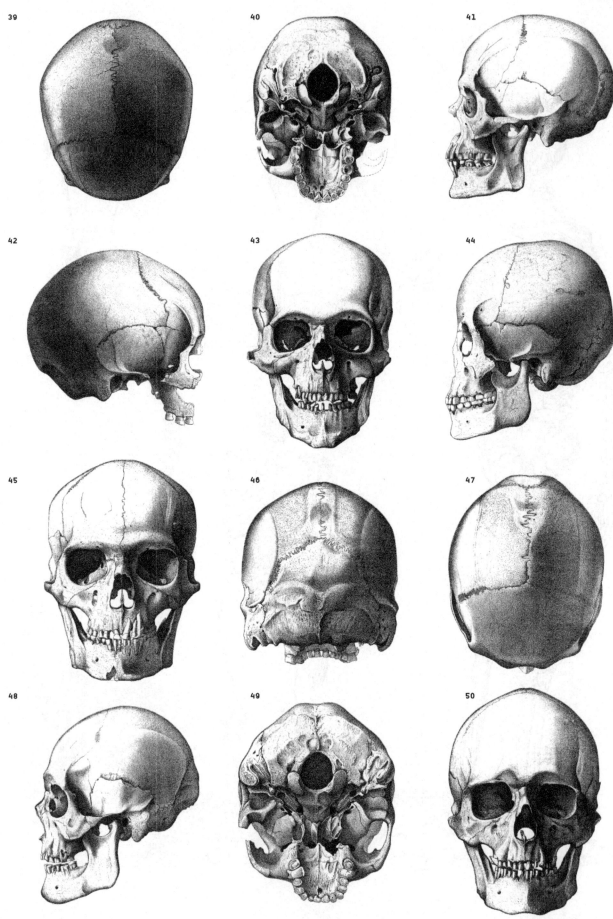

39

40

41

42

43

44

45

46

47

48

49

50

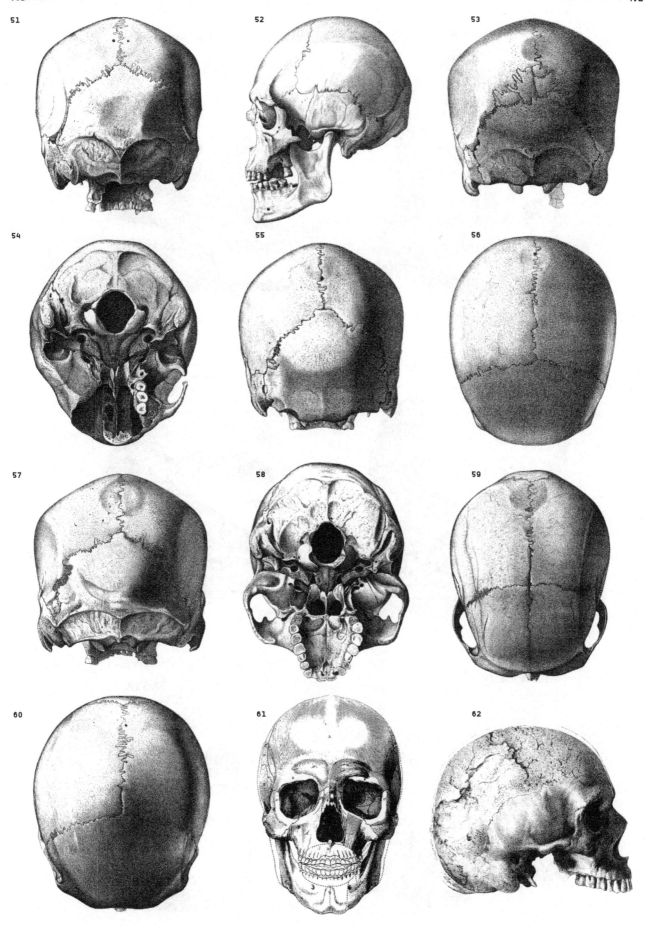

51

52

53

54

55

56

57

58

59

60

61

62

63

FIGVRA PRIMA

FIGVRA SECONDA

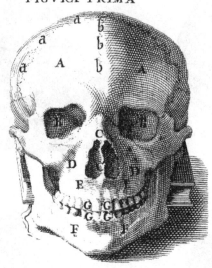
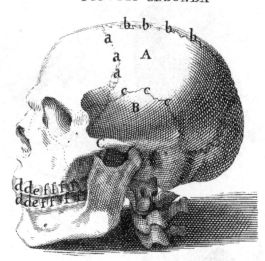

FIGVRA TERZA

FIGVRA QVARTA

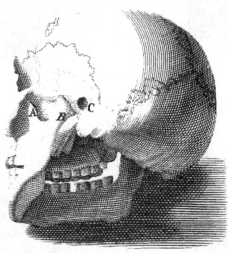
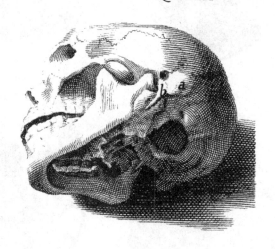

FIGVRA QVINTA

FIGVRA SESTA.

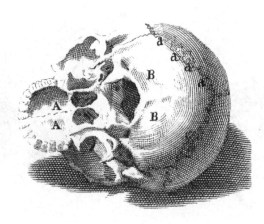
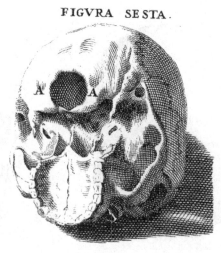

FIG I

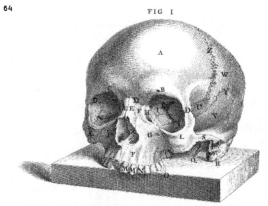

FIG II

FIG III

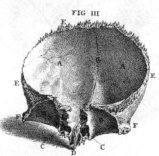

FIG I

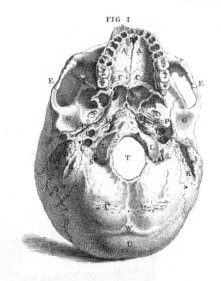

FIG III

FIG II

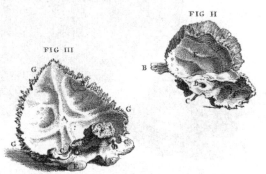

FIG I

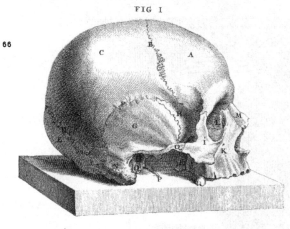

FIG II

FIG III

FIG IIII

FIG V

FIG VI

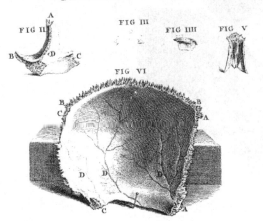

FIG I

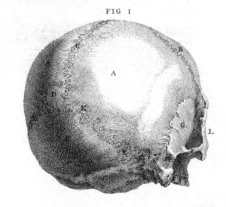

FIG II

FIG III

FIG V

FIG IIII

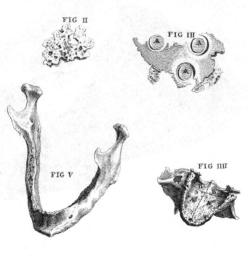

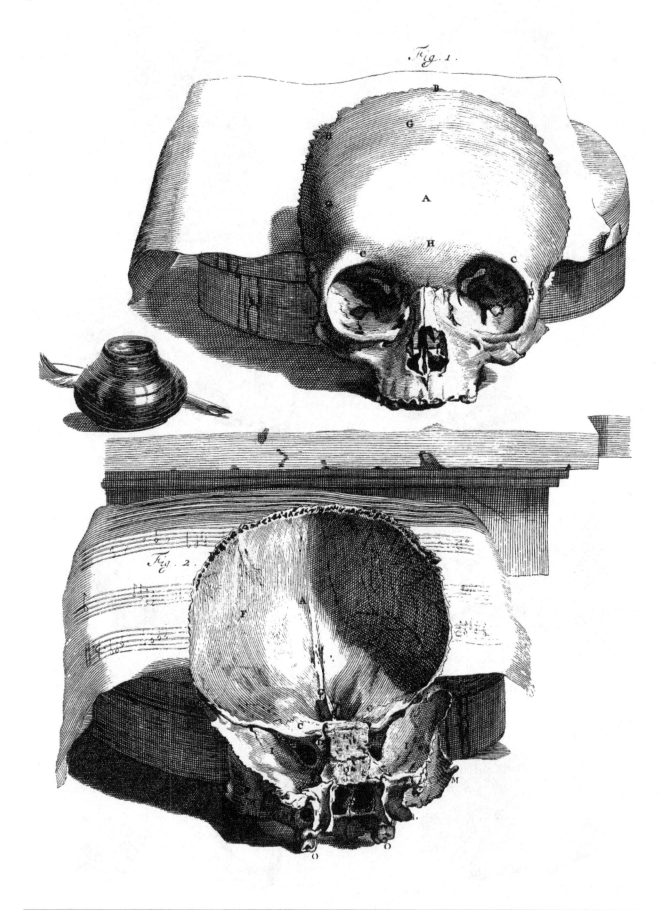

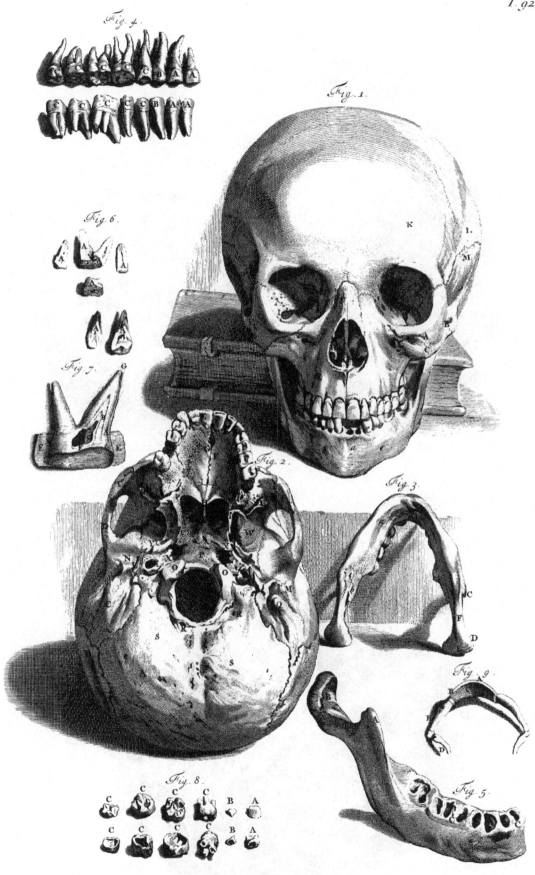

XLII

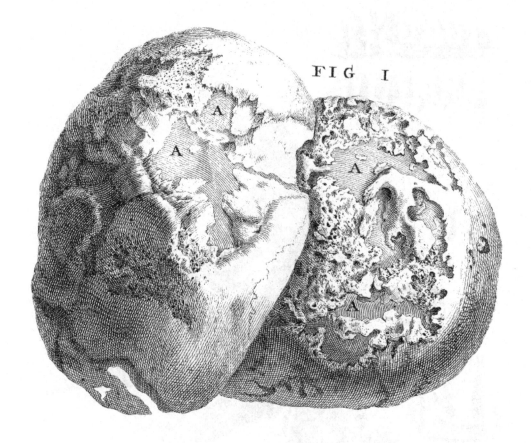

FIG I

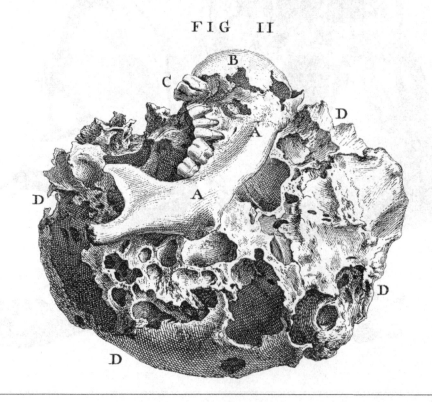

FIG II

XLI

FIG I

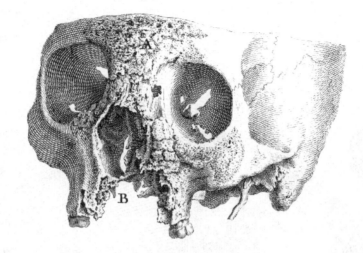

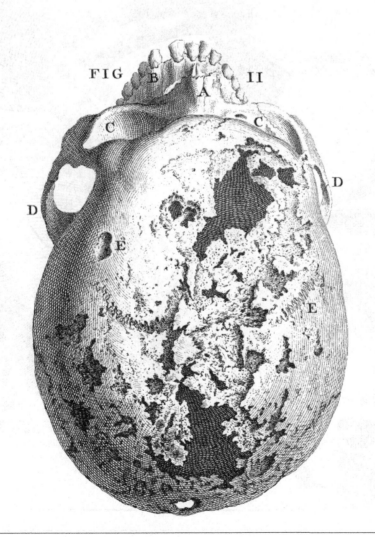

FIG II

72

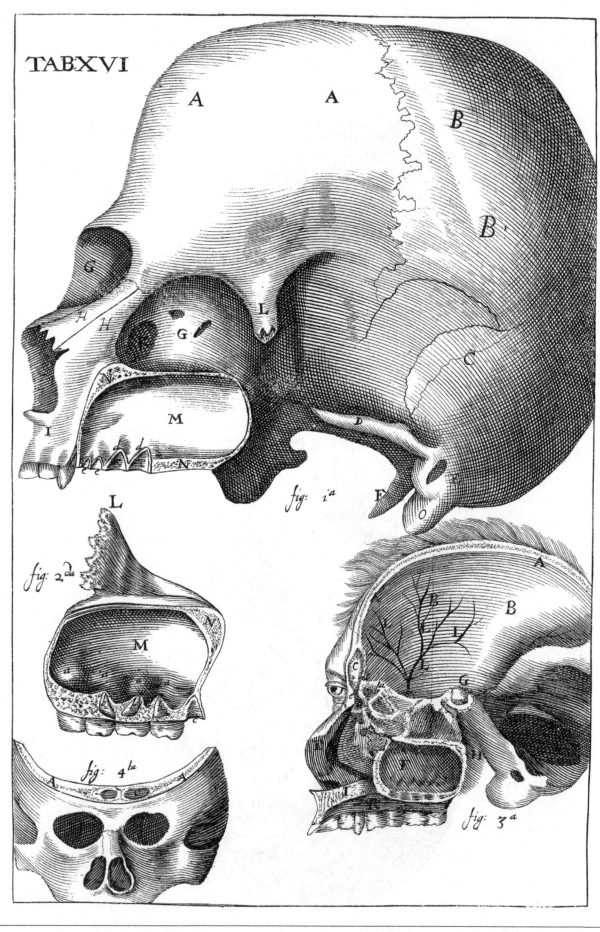

TAB·XVI

fig: 1ª

fig: 2ᵈª

fig: 4ˡª

fig: 3ª

73

74

75

76

77

78

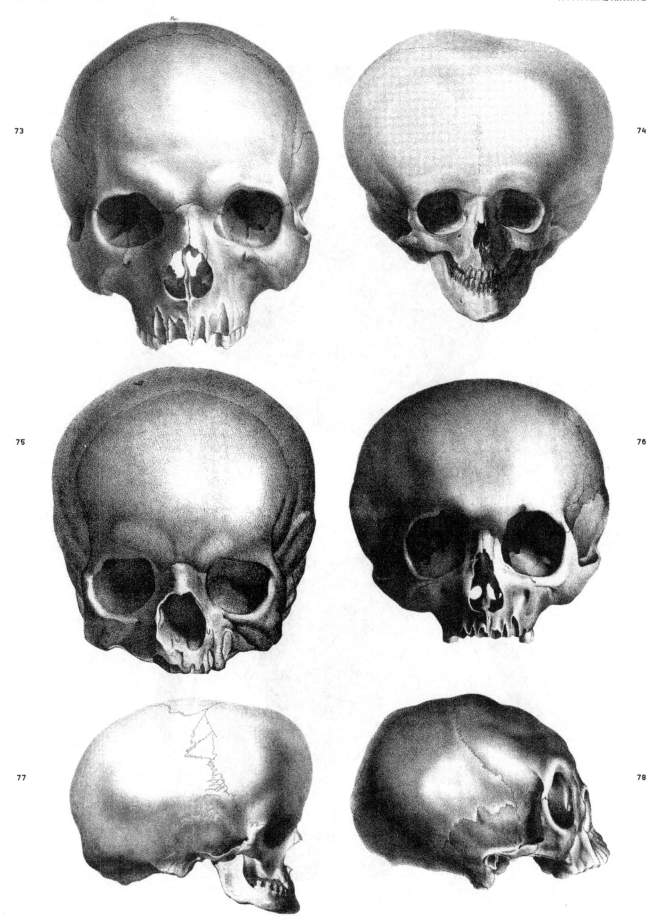

SKULLS AND SKELETONS

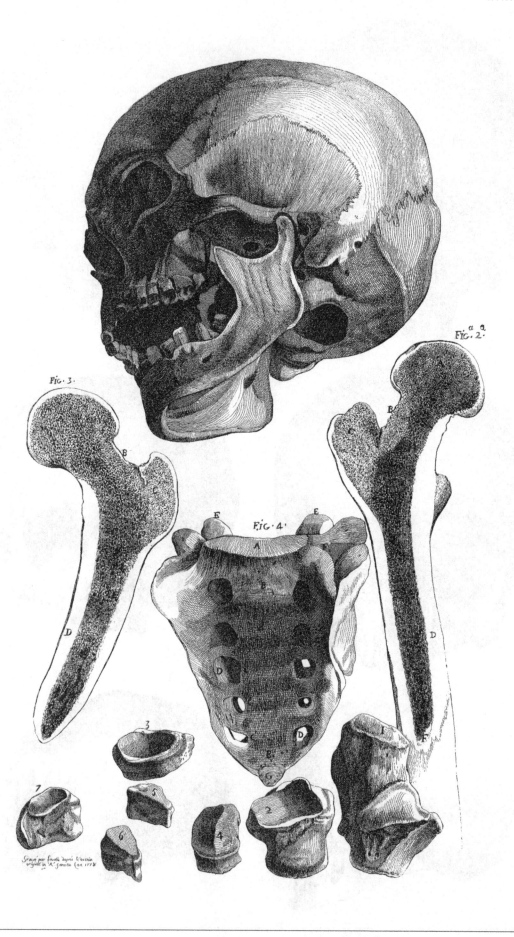

FIG. 2.

FIG. 3.

FIG. 4.

80

81

82

83

84

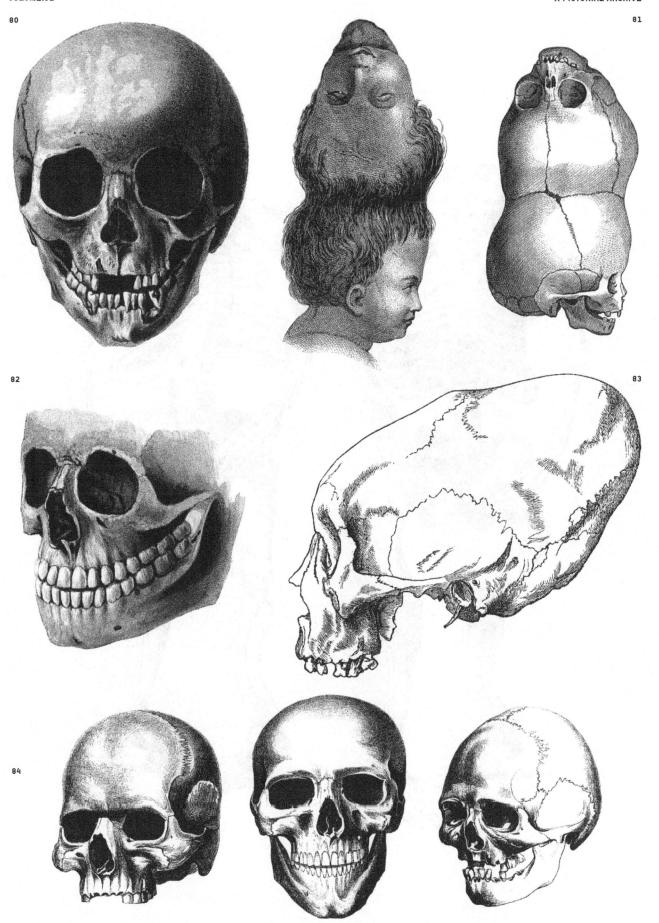

SKULLS AND SKELETONS

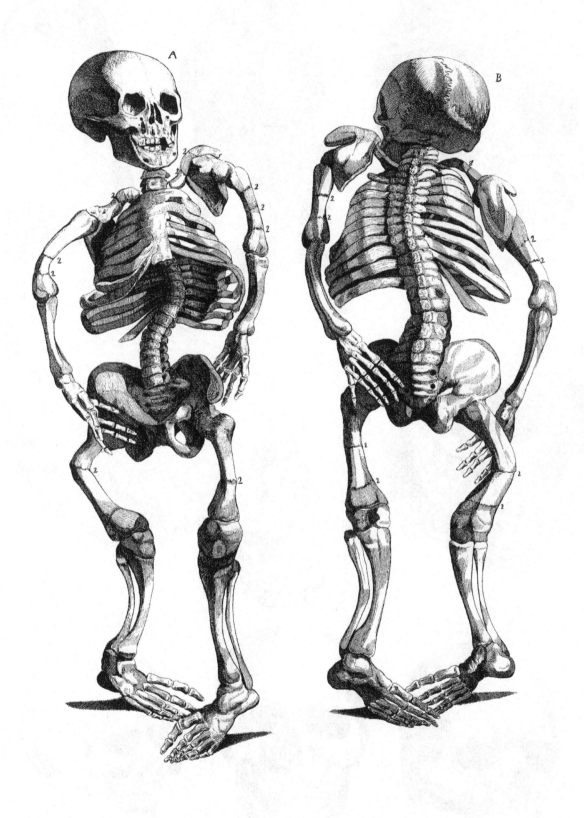

86

87

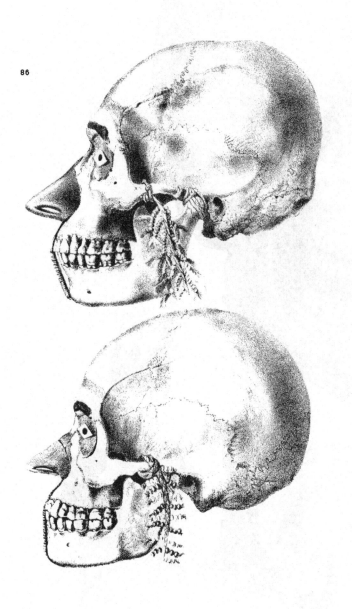

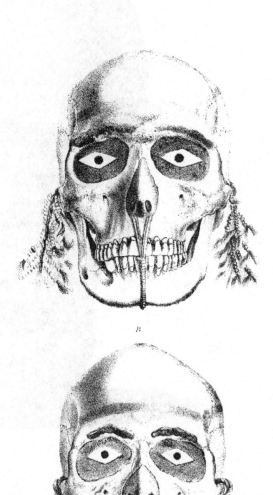

B.

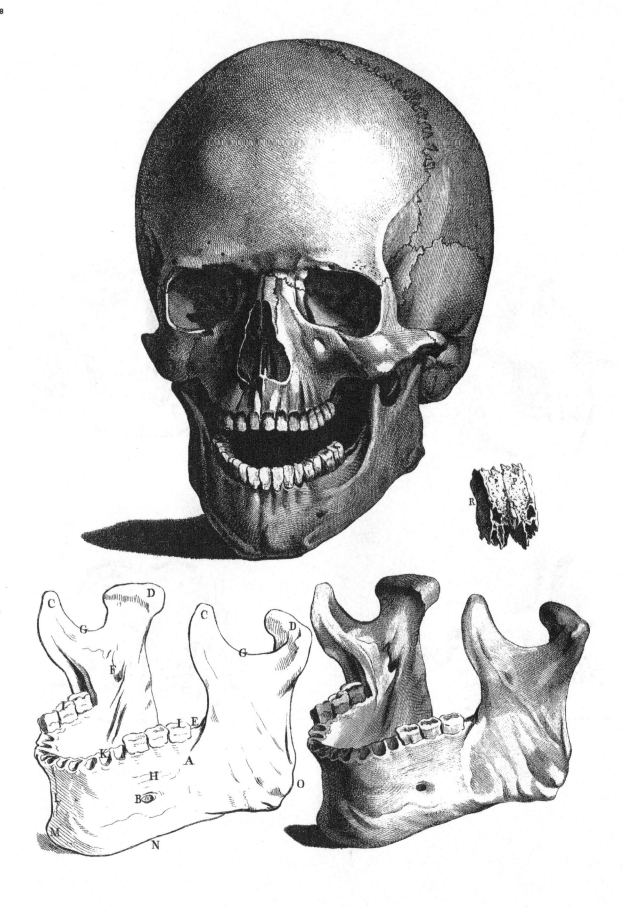

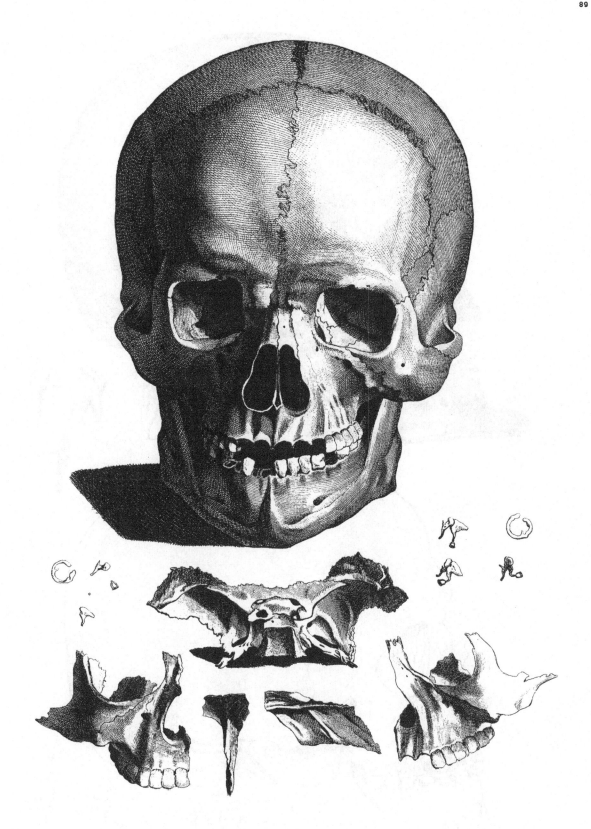

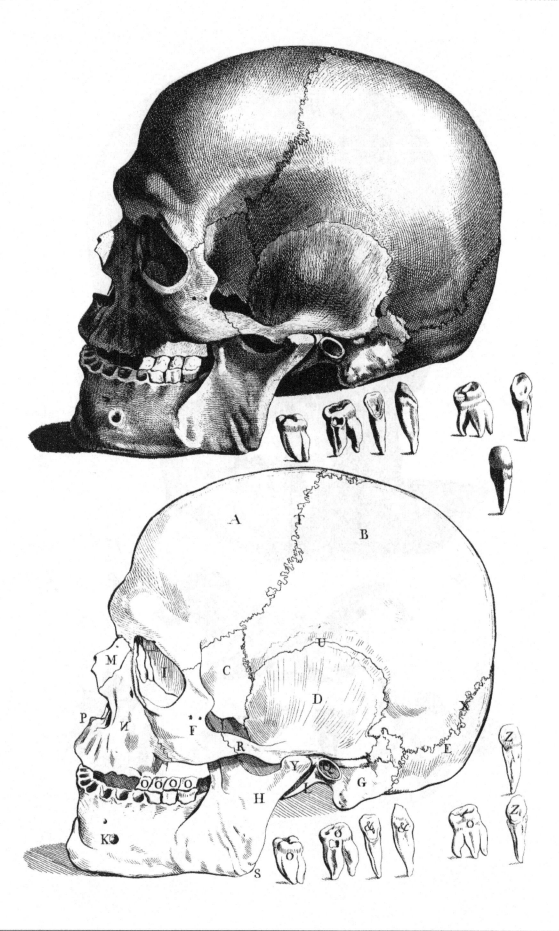

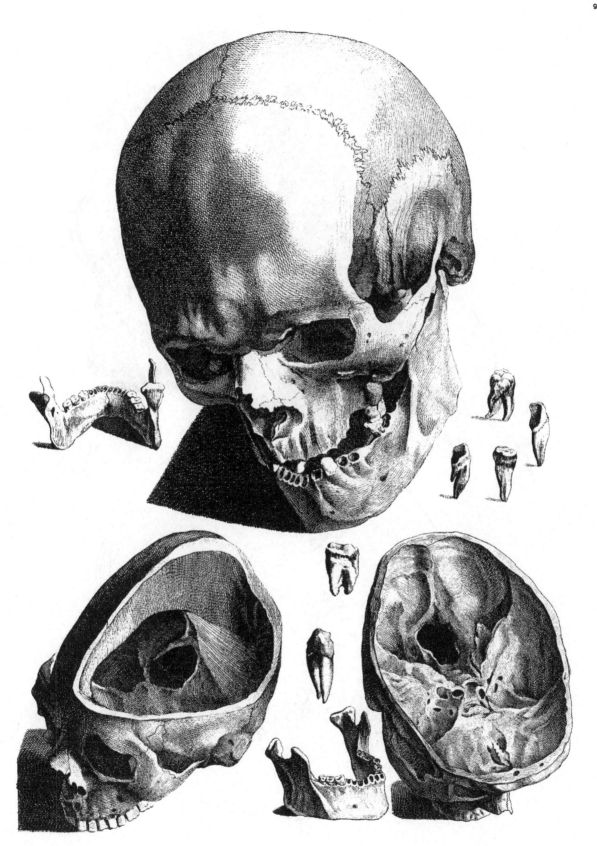

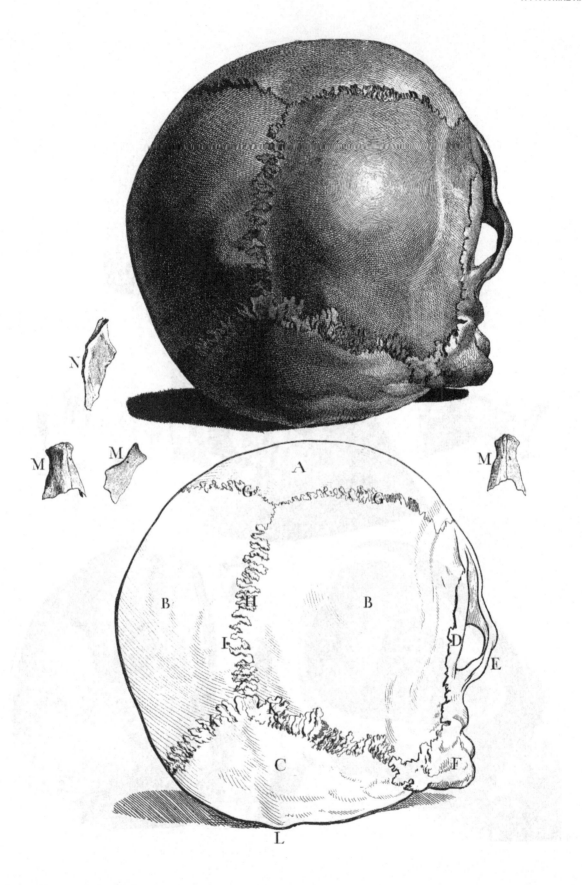

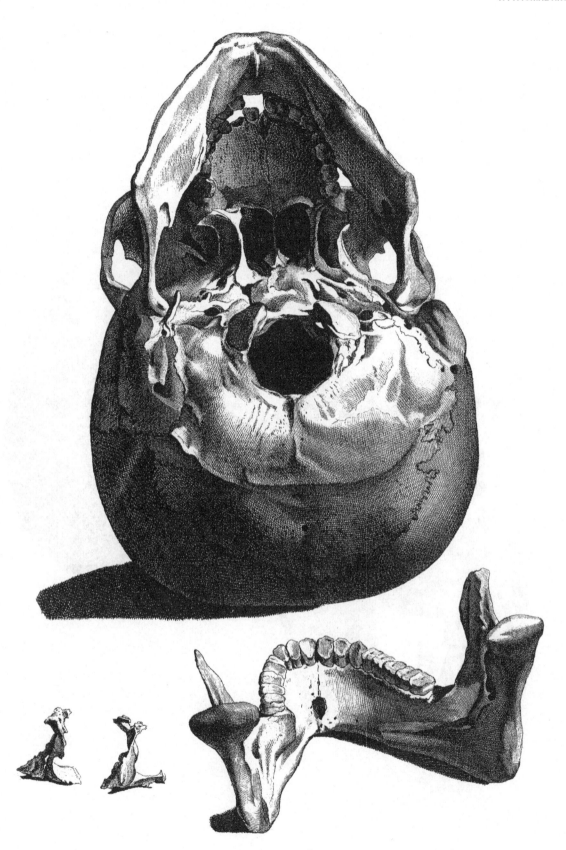

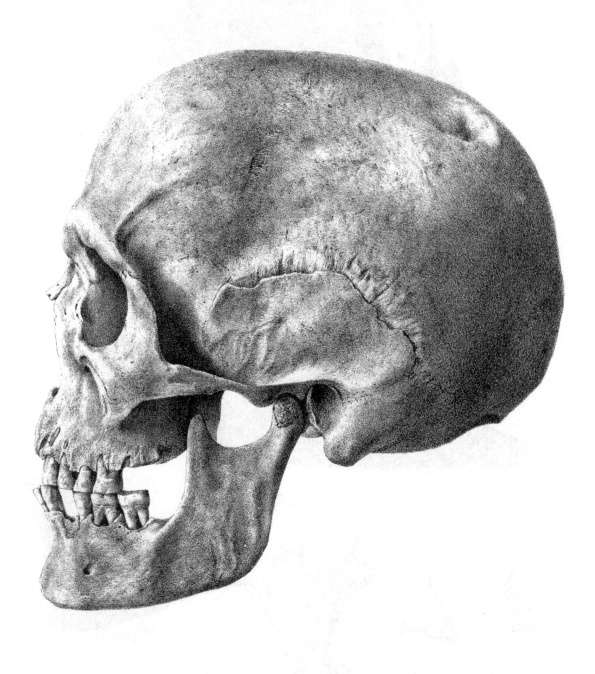

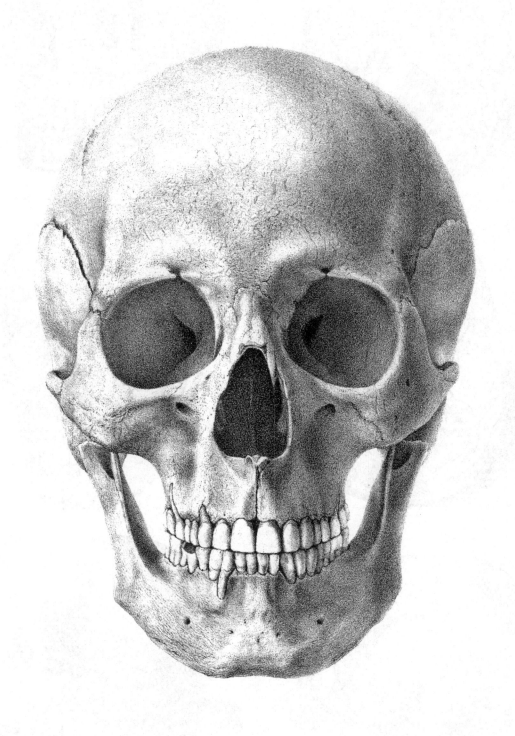

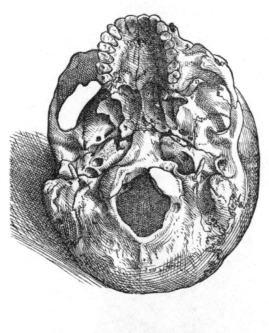

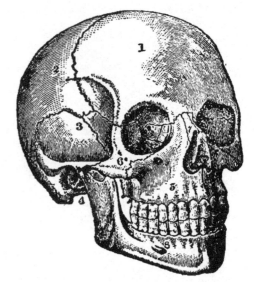

FIG. 4.

SKULLS AND SKELETONS

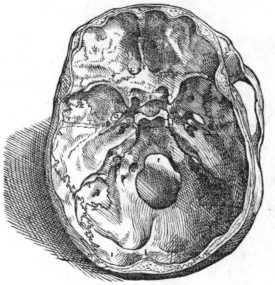

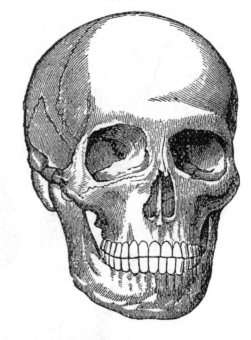

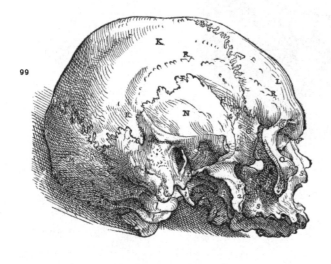

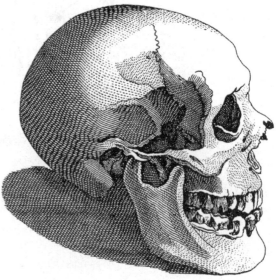

101

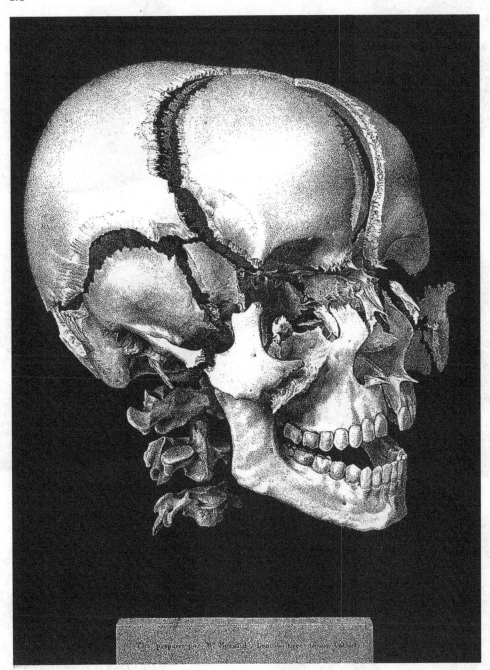

Tete preparee par M. Morand. Dentiste (type de son Cabinet)

102

103

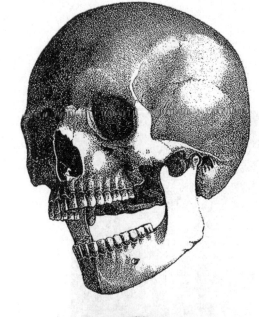

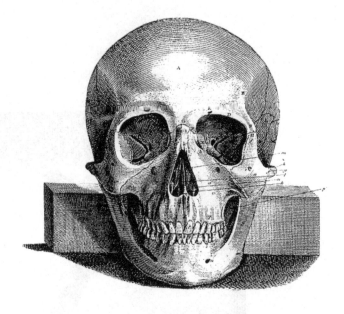

SKULLS AND SKELETONS

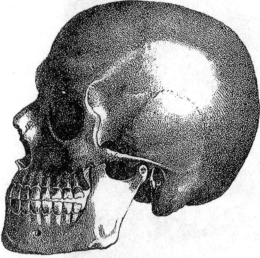

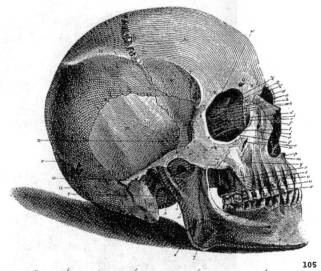

104

105

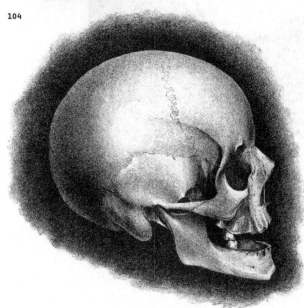

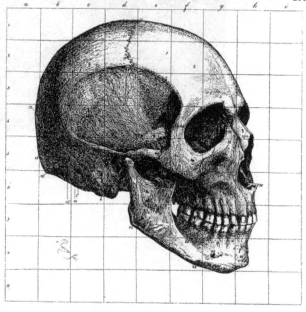

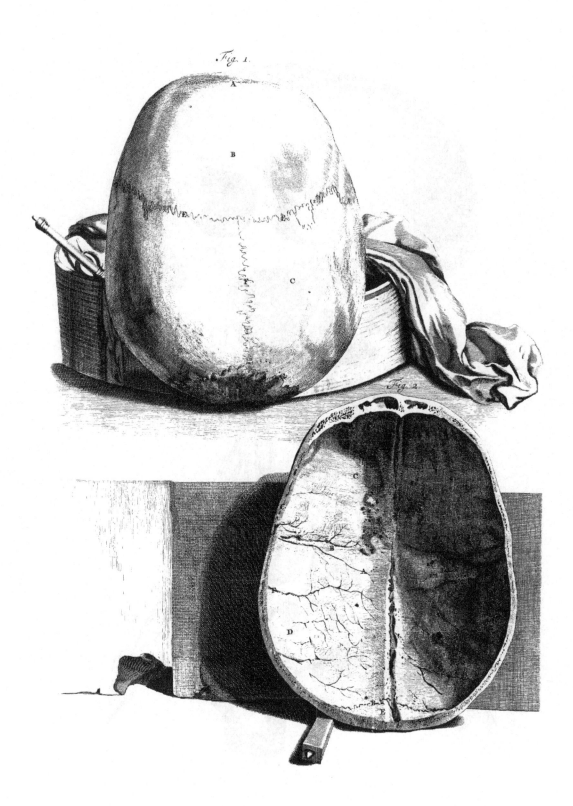

SKULLS AND SKELETONS

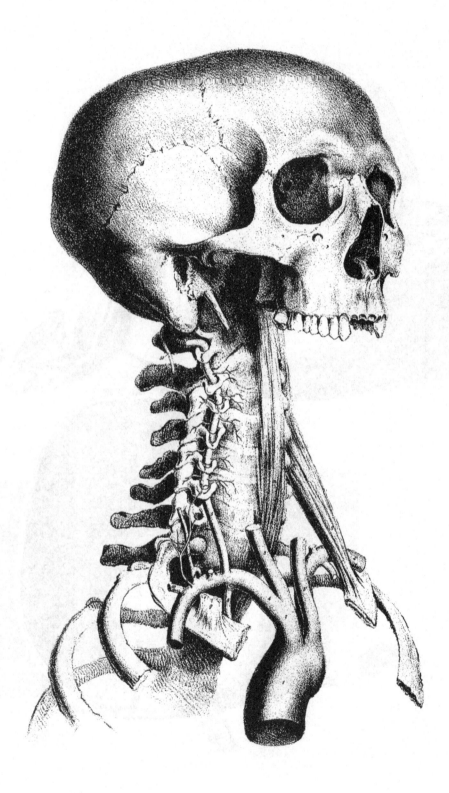

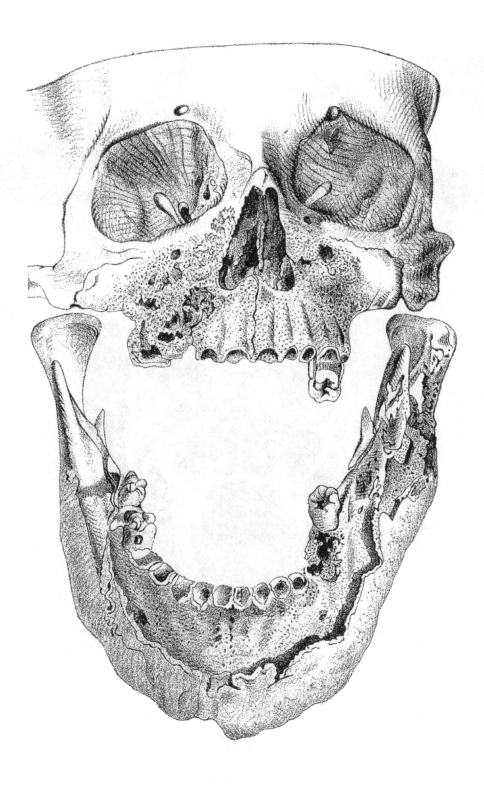

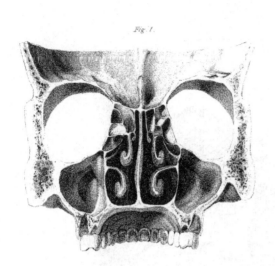

Fig. 1.

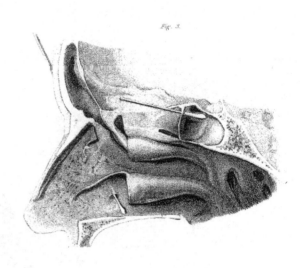

Fig. 3.

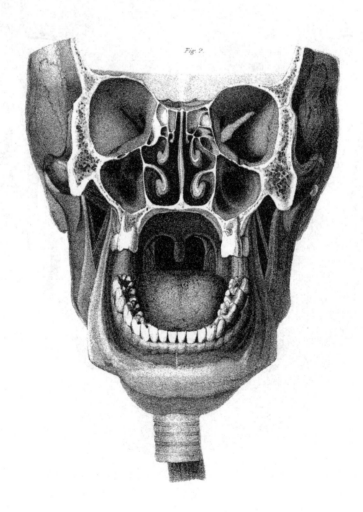

Fig. 2.

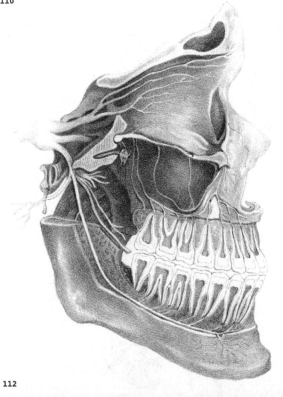

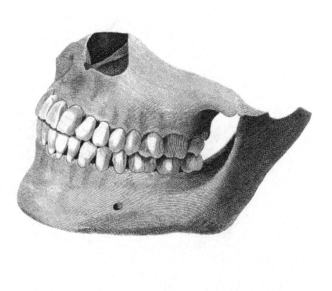

112

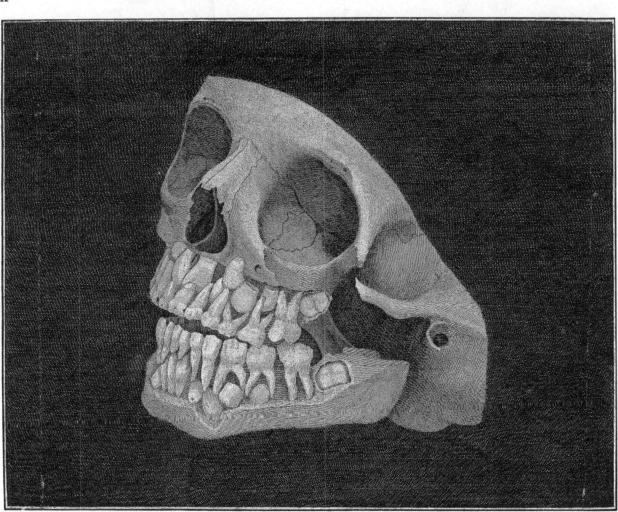

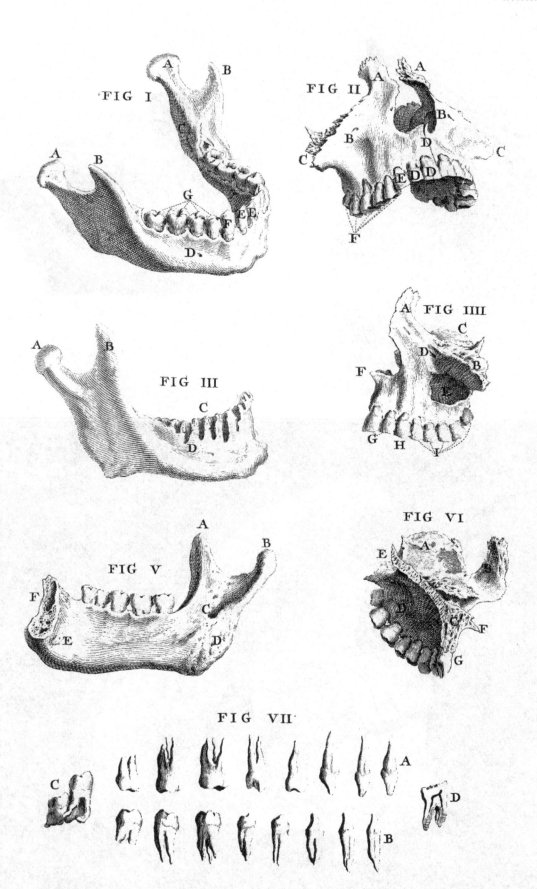

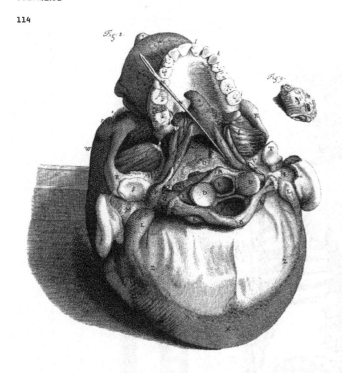

FIG I

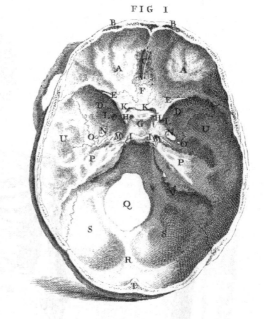

Fig.1.

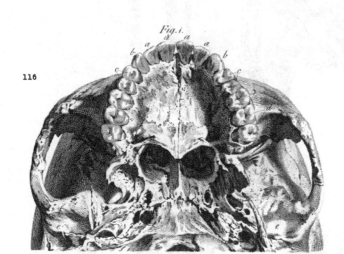

FIG II

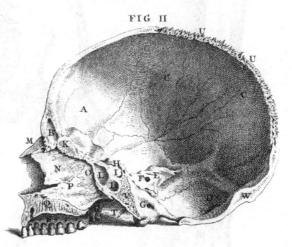

SKULLS AND SKELETONS

Fig.2.

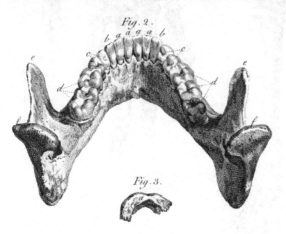

Fig.3.

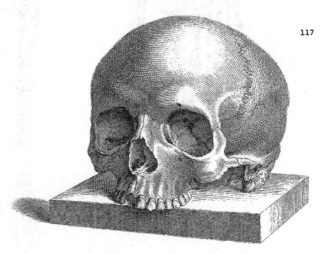

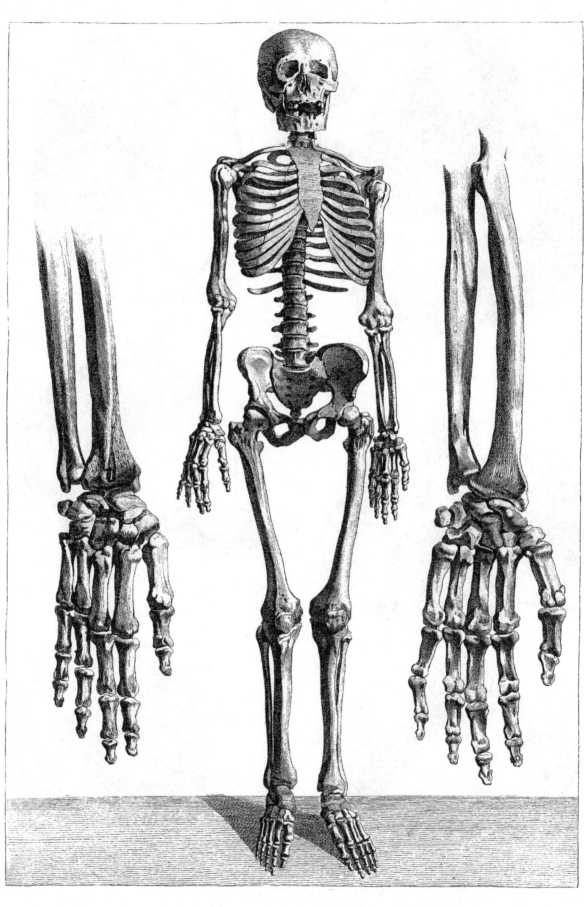

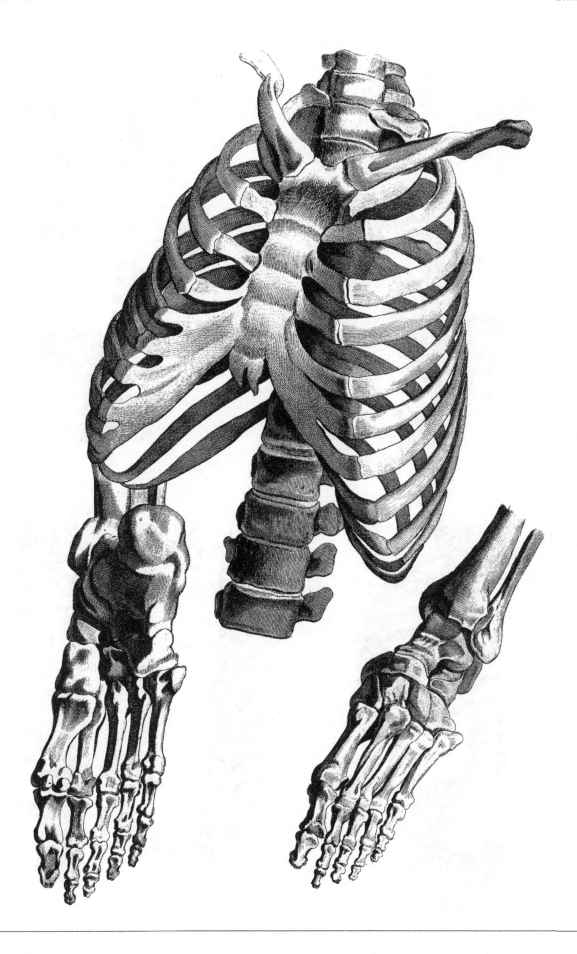

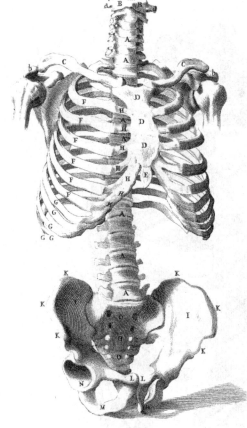

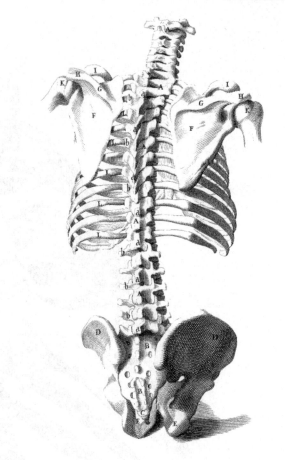

SKULLS AND SKELETONS

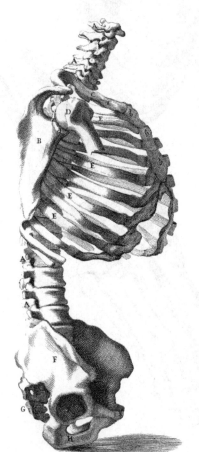

FIG II

FIG I

FIG III

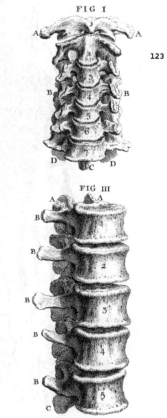

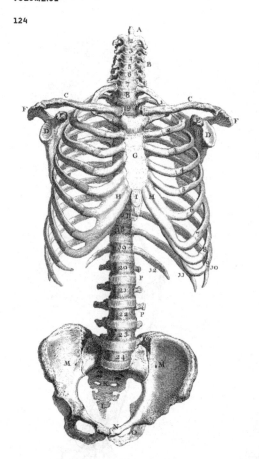

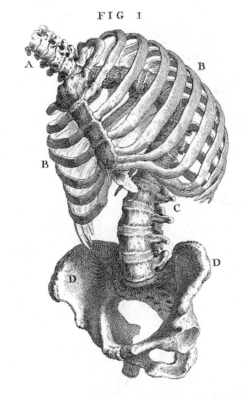

FIG I

XX

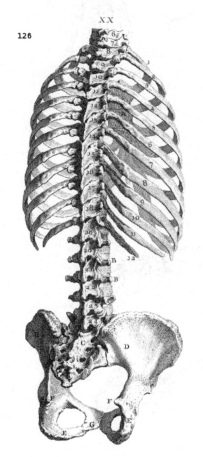

FIG II

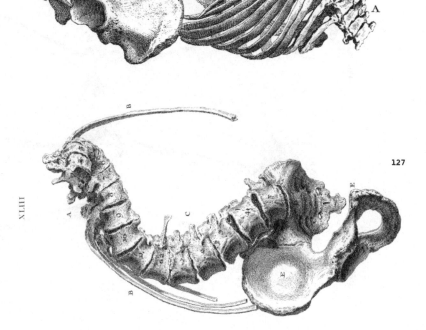

XLIII

SKULLS AND SKELETONS

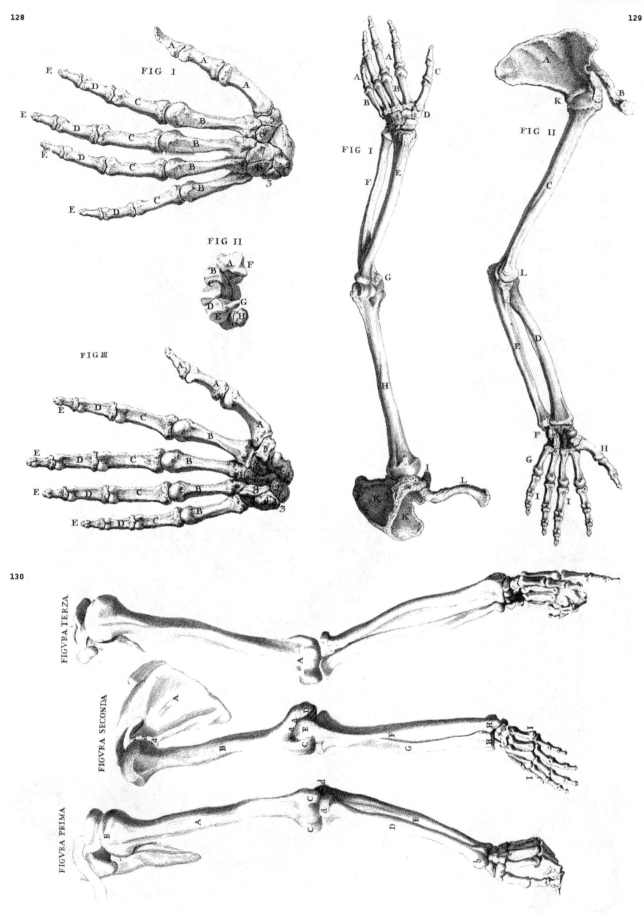

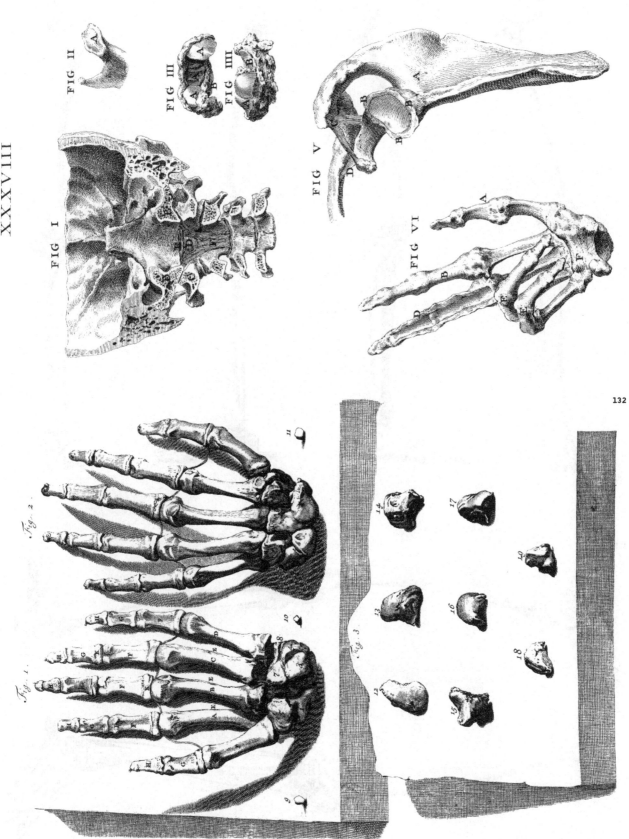

SKULLS AND SKELETONS

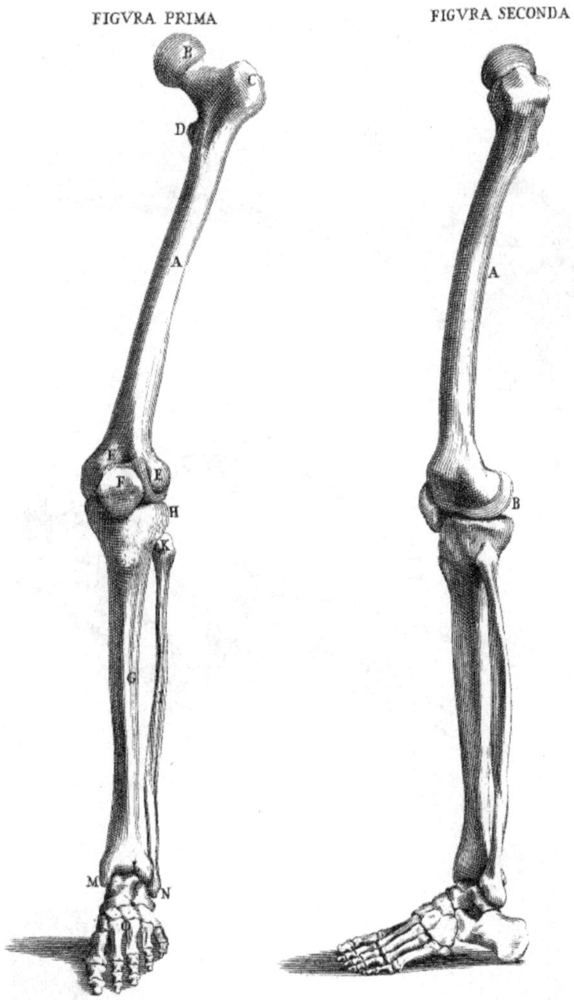

FIGVRA PRIMA

FIGVRA SECONDA

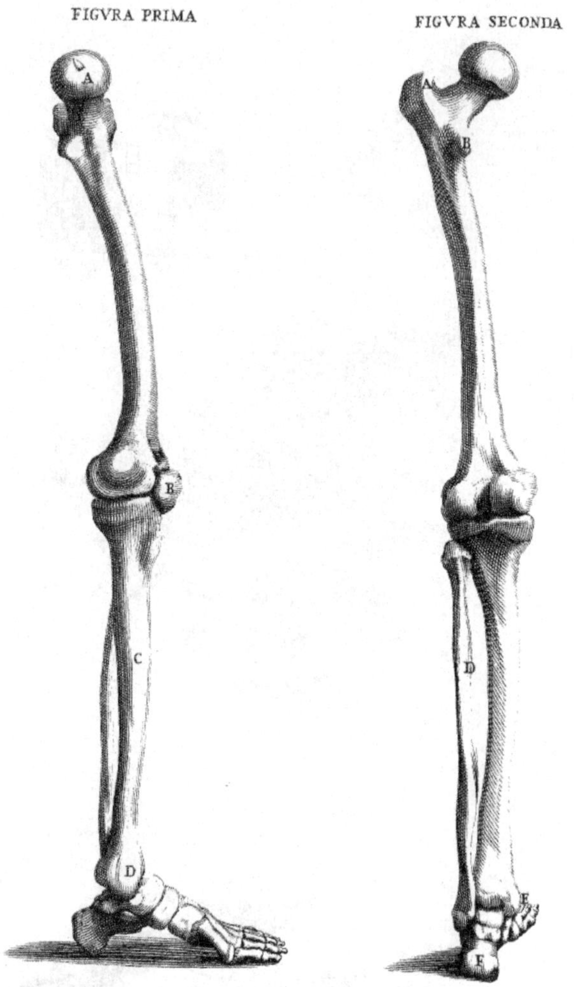

FIGVRA PRIMA

FIGVRA SECONDA

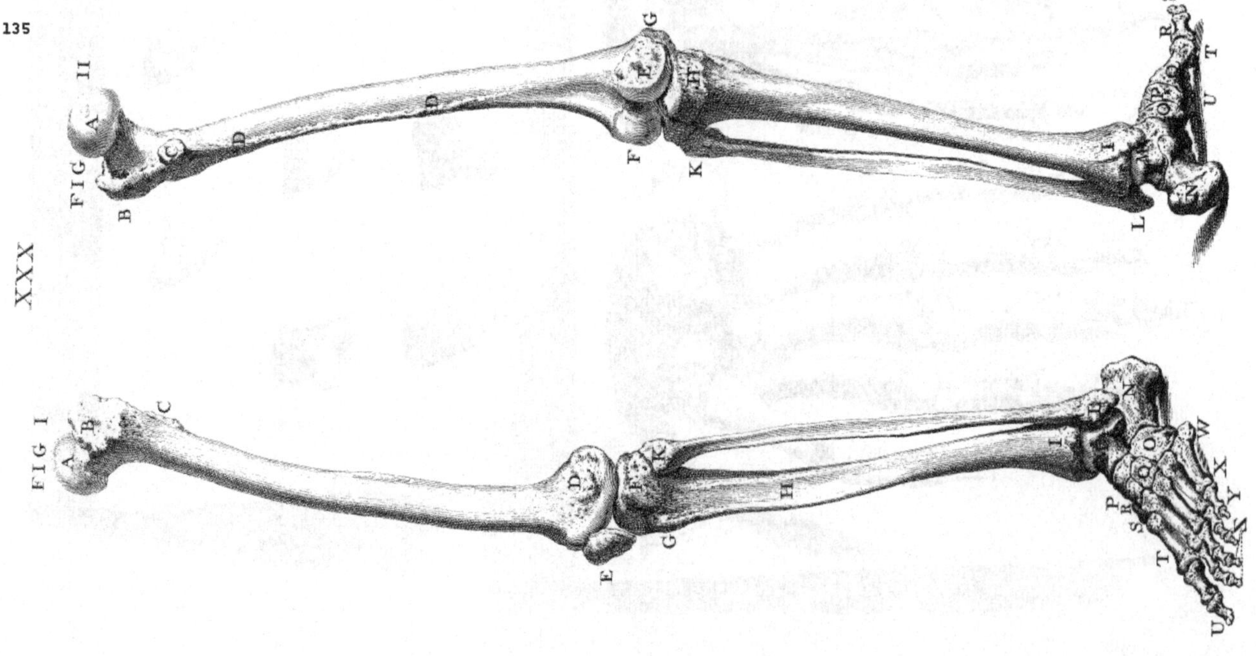

XXX

FIG II

FIG I

XXIX

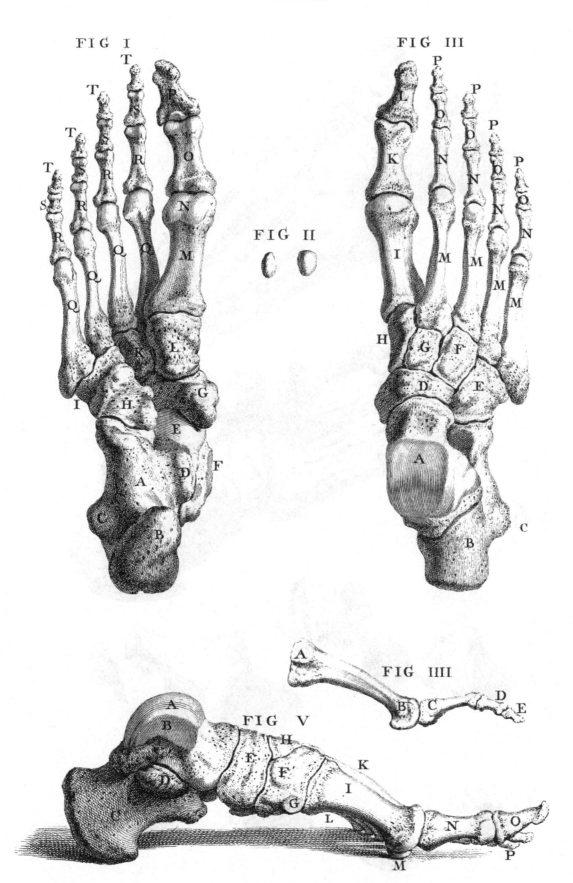

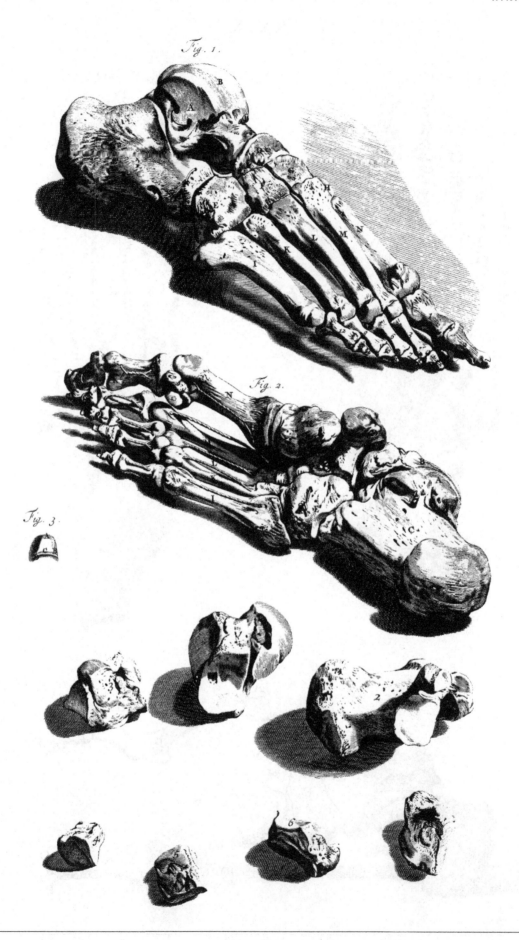

Fig. 1.

Fig. 2.

Fig. 3.

TAVOLA NONA

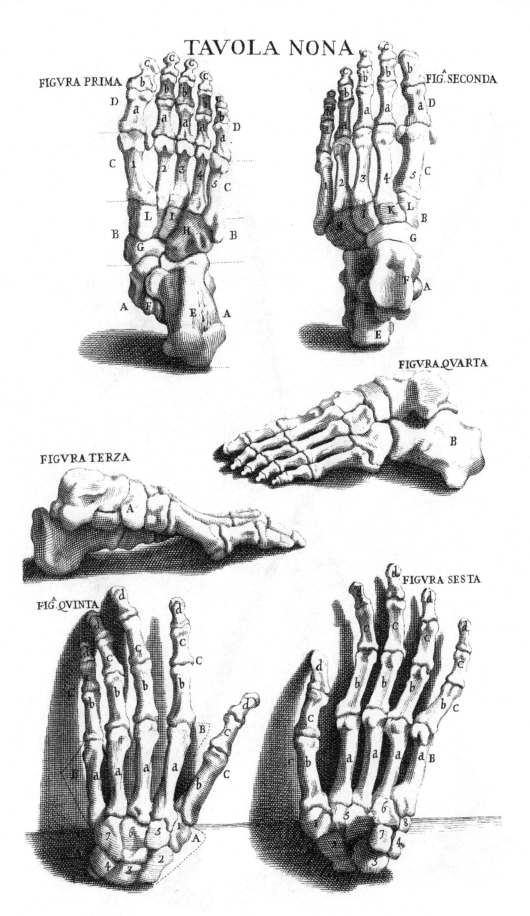

139

XXVII

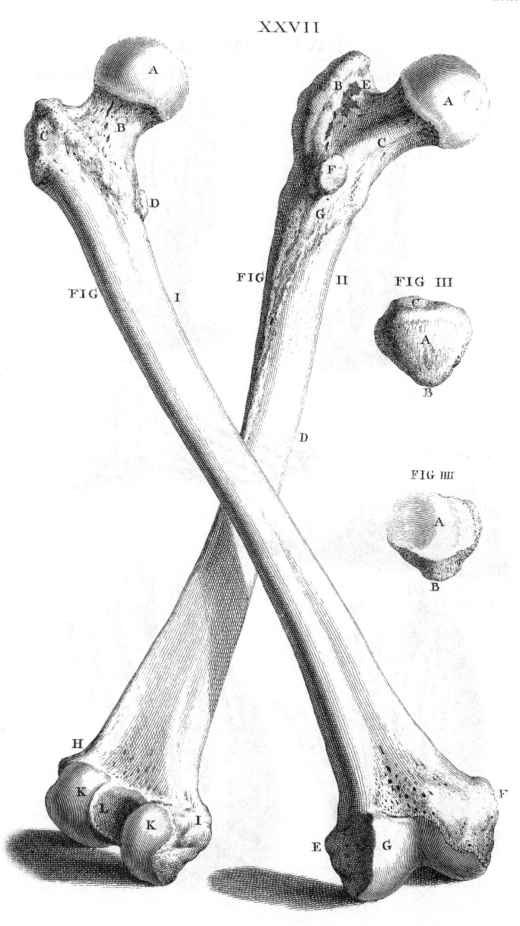

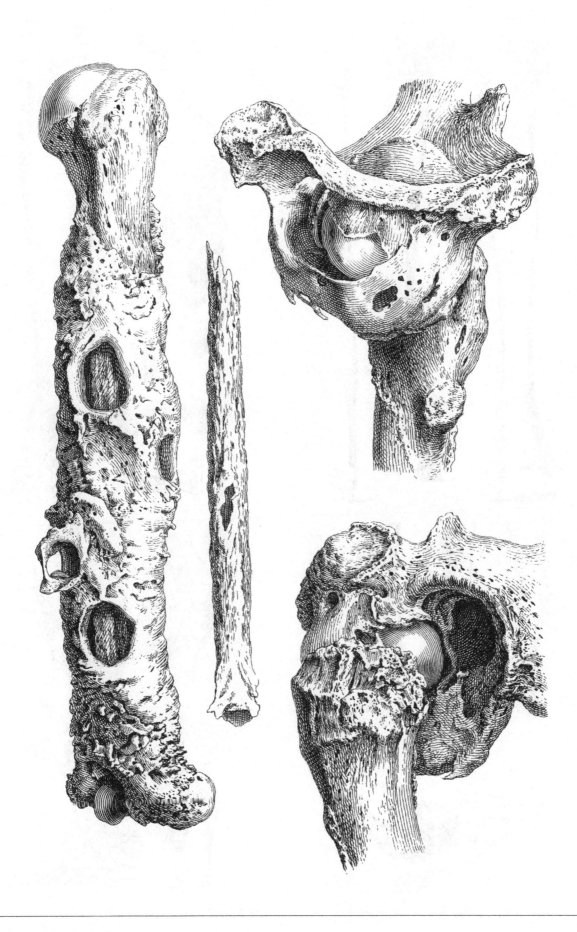

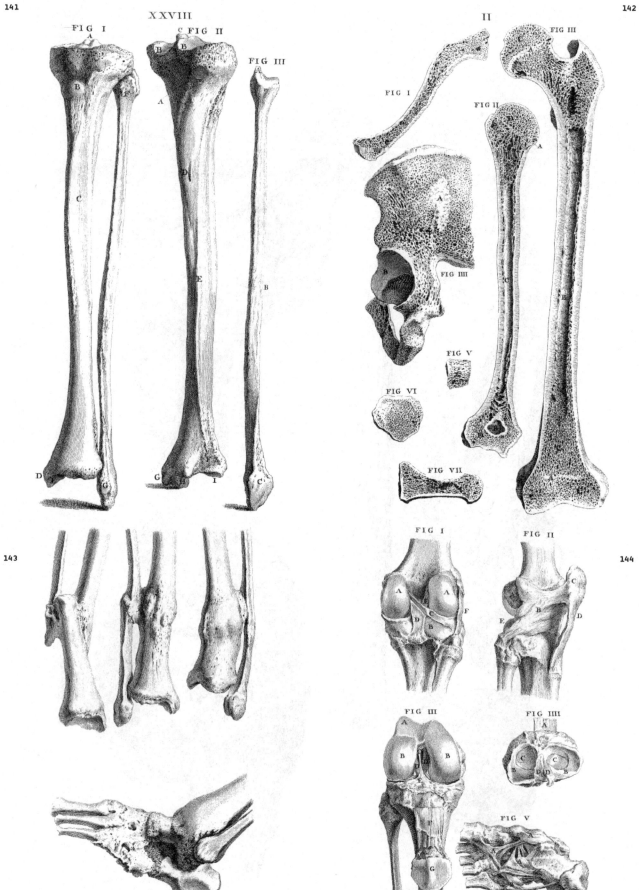

XXXIX

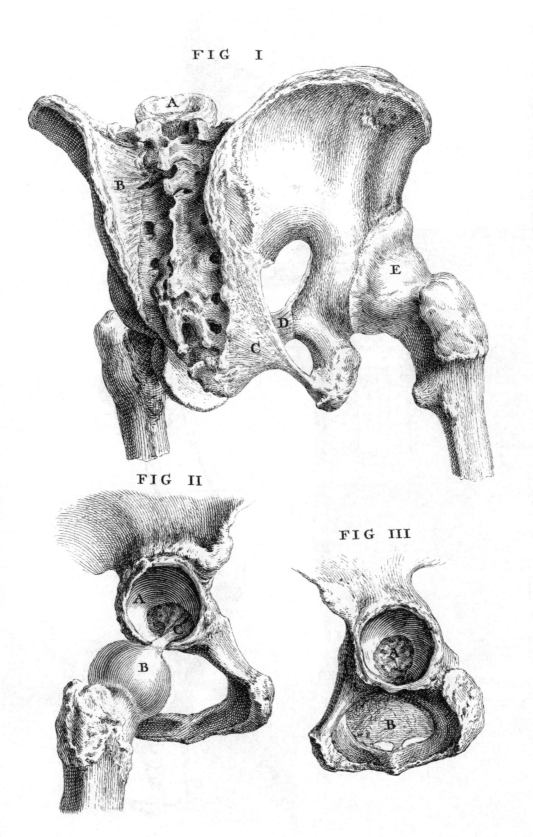

FIG I

FIG II

FIG III

146

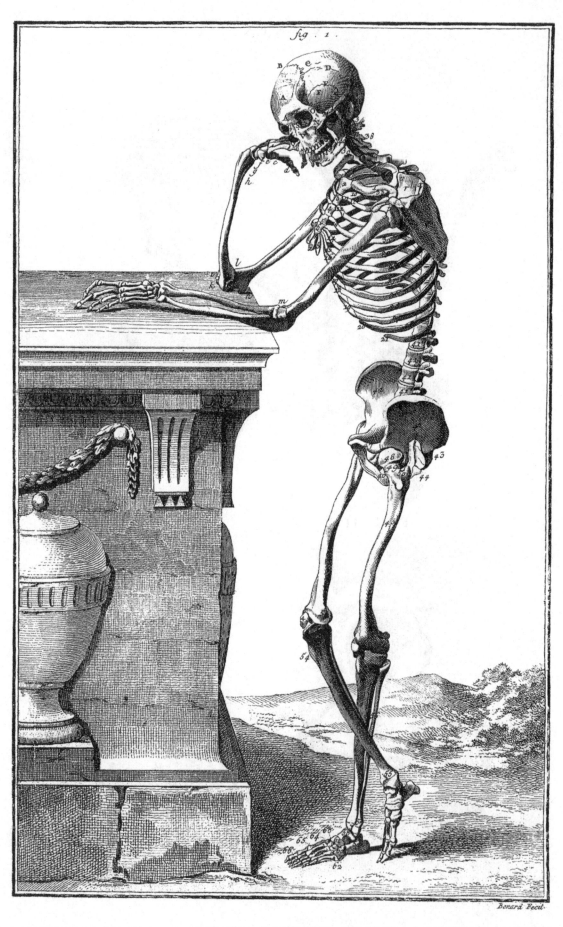

Bonard Fecit.

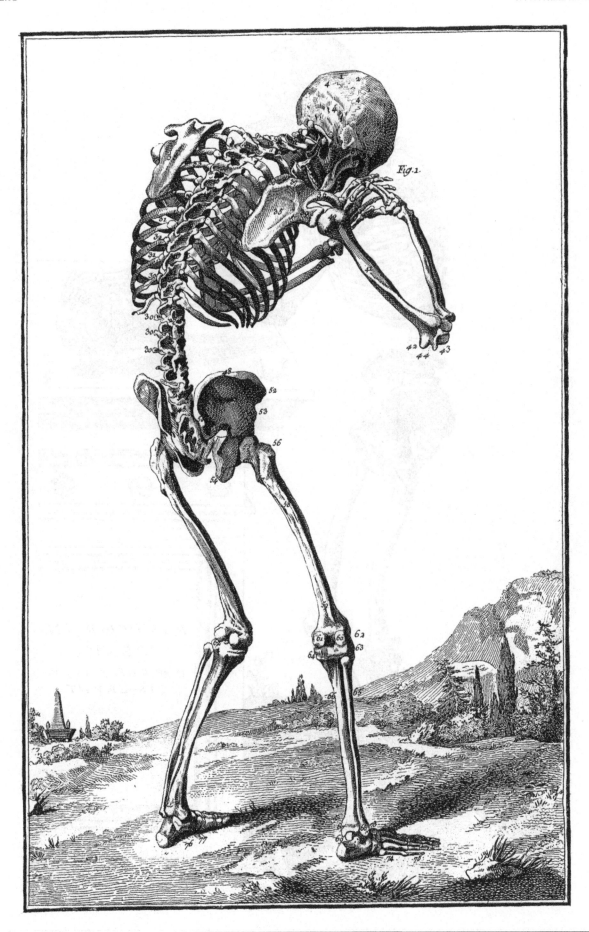

Fig.1.

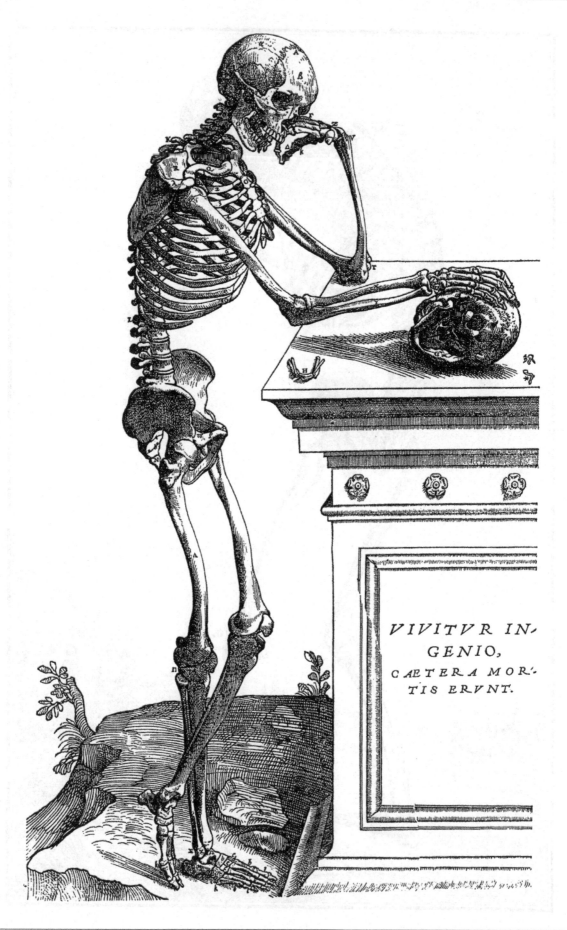

VIVITVR IN-
GENIO,
CÆTERA MOR-
TIS ERVNT.

149

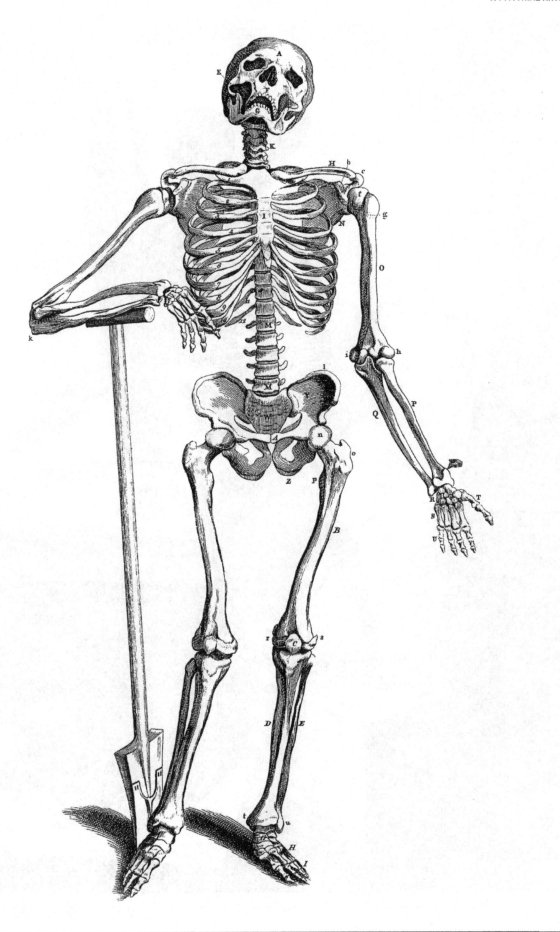

150

permis d'imprimer
Lartigue fugem...

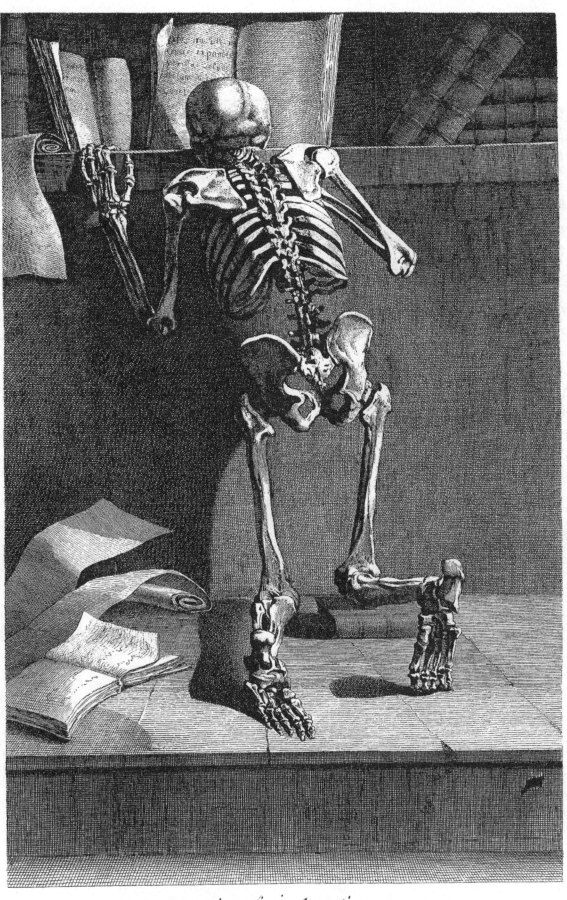

Orate ne intretis in tentationem

SED ARX TUTA EST MORTIS AB IMPERIO. SIVE SUMUS

FORTE LOCUS DABITUR CONTRA OMNIA CÆTERA TUTUS: NULLA

SCEPTRO INSIGNES, SIVE ARVA LIGONE PERFODIMUS, ΘΑΝΑΤΩ ΓΑΝΤ ΕΣ ΟΦΕΙΛΟΜΕΘΑ.

(ἔκτοϛ) ΘΝΑΤΑ΄ ΜΕΜΝΑ΄ΣΘΩ ΓΕΡΙΣ Τ Ε΄ΛΛΩΝ ΜΕΛΗ. Pindarus

154

155

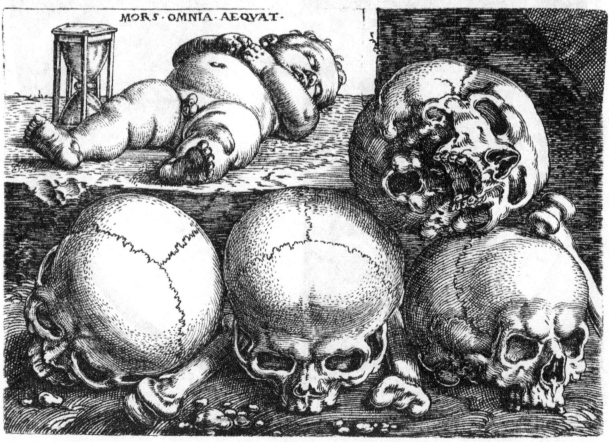

156

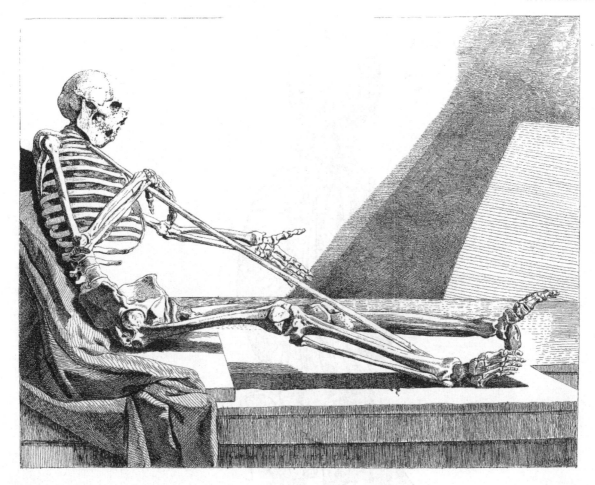

157

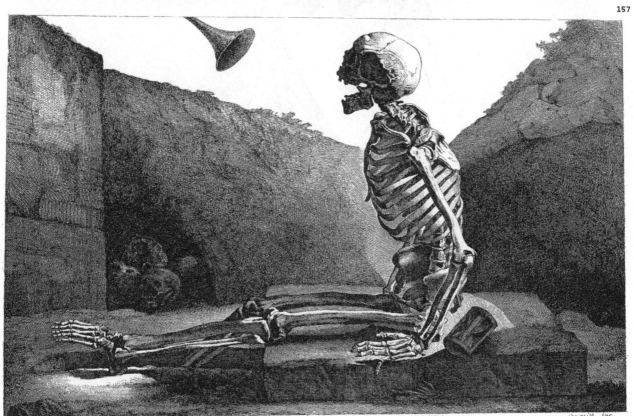

Surqite mortui venite ad Judicium

158

208

DECIMA
QVARTA
MVSCVLO-
RVM TA-
BVLA.

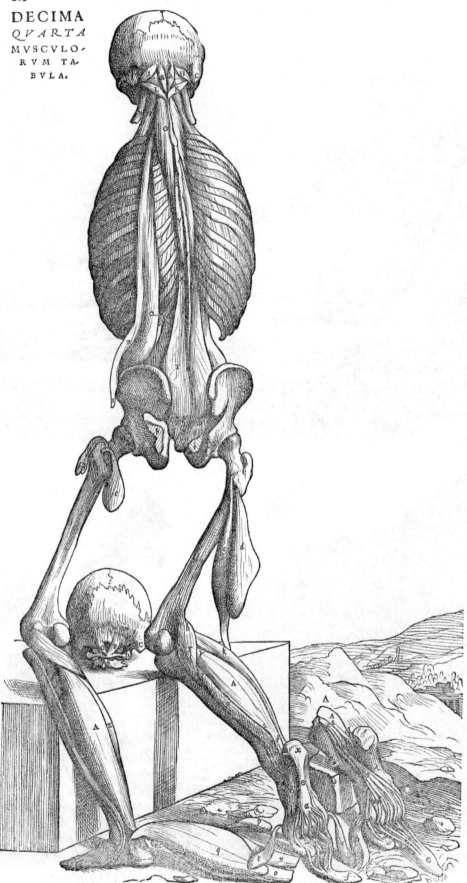

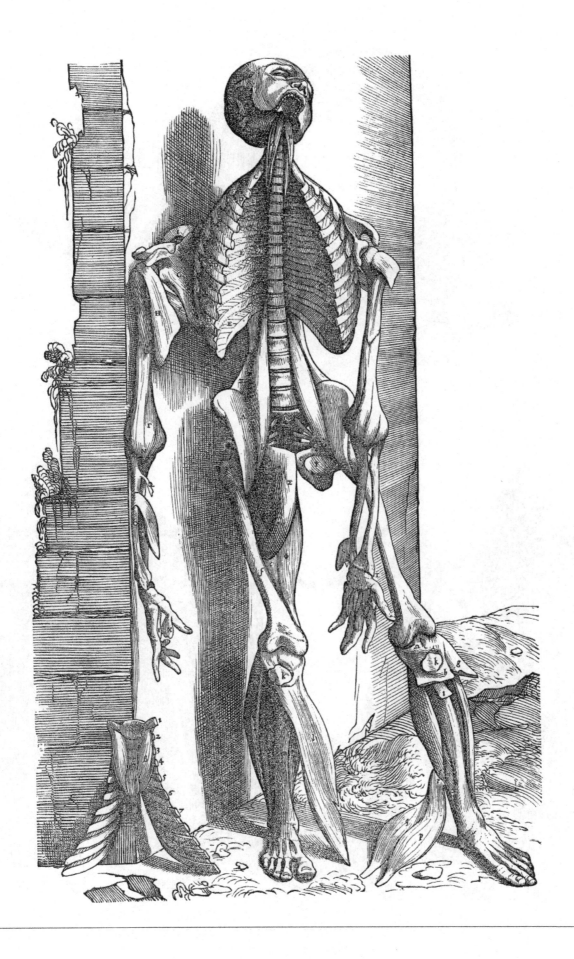

160

161

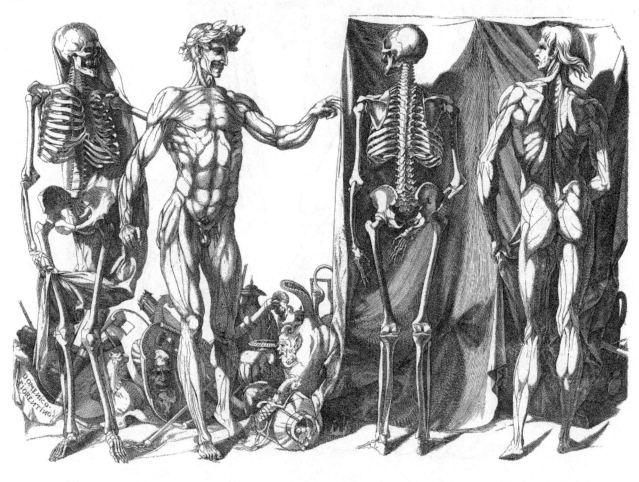

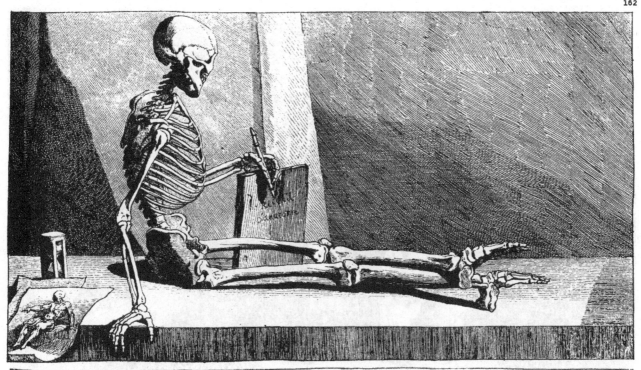

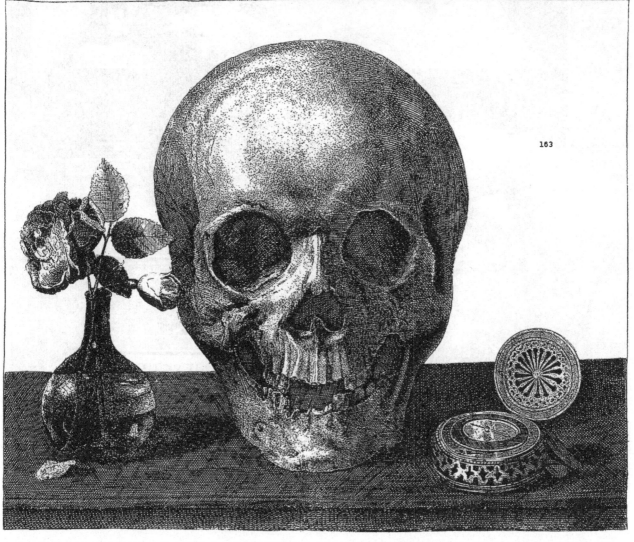

SKULLS AND SKELETONS

164

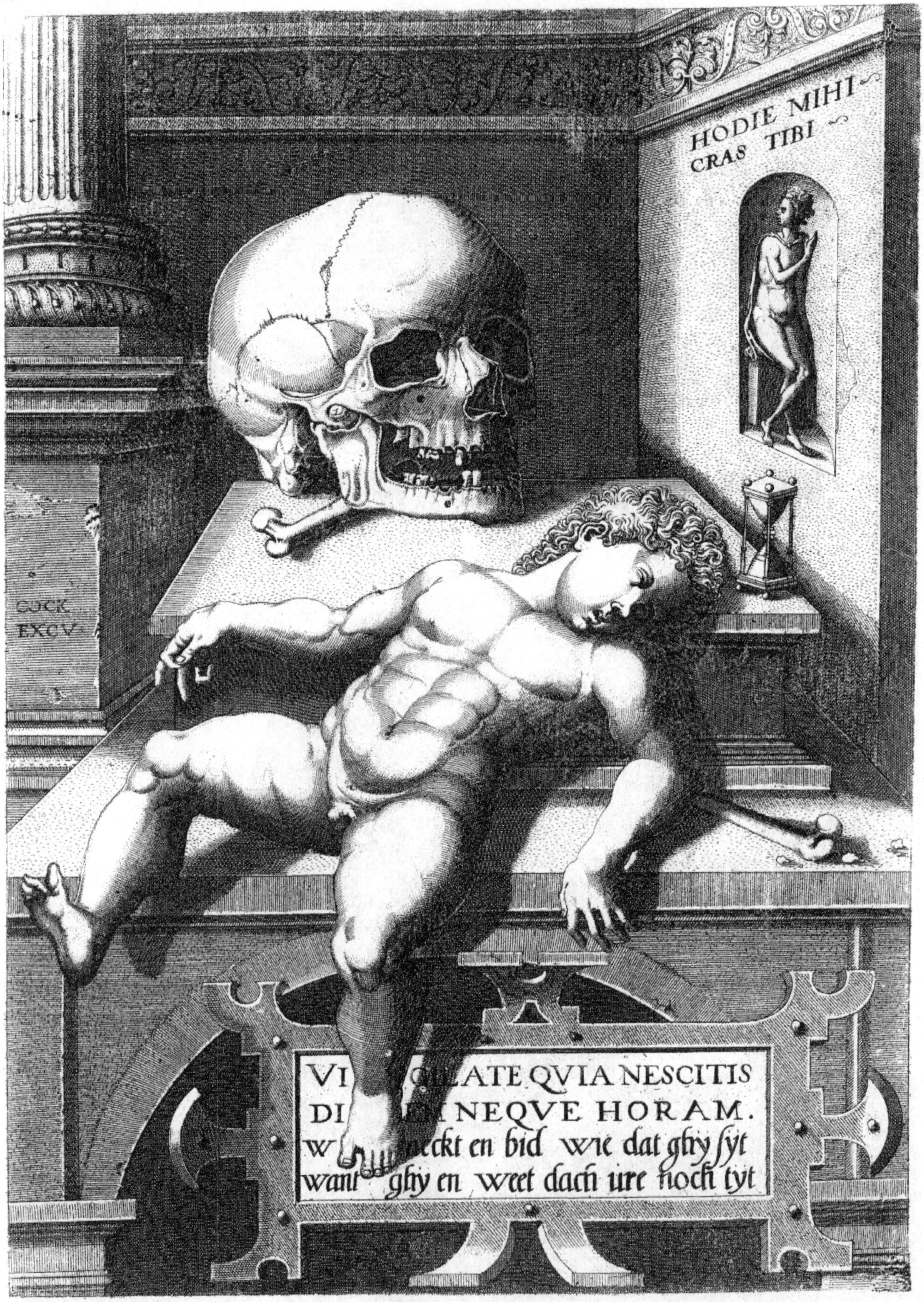

HODIE MIHI
CRAS TIBI

COCK
EXCV

VI... ...ILATE QVIA NESCITIS
DI... ...NEQVE HORAM.
w... ...eckt en bid wie dat ghy syt
want ghy en weet dach ure noch tyt

166

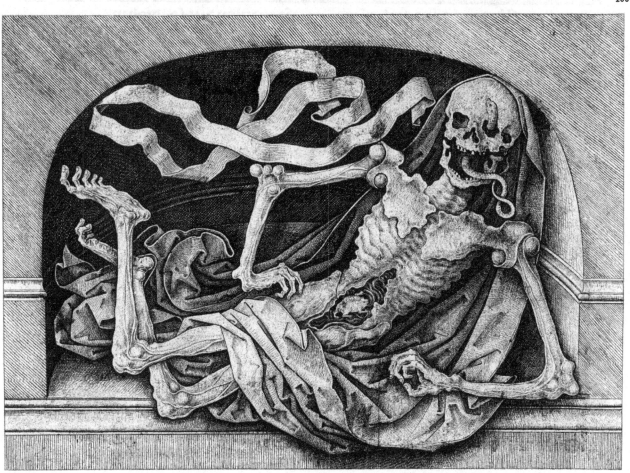

167

Ghedenckt op u uytersten/
UUie dat ghy zijt/

Soo zuldy niet sondighen/
Tot geender tijt.

168

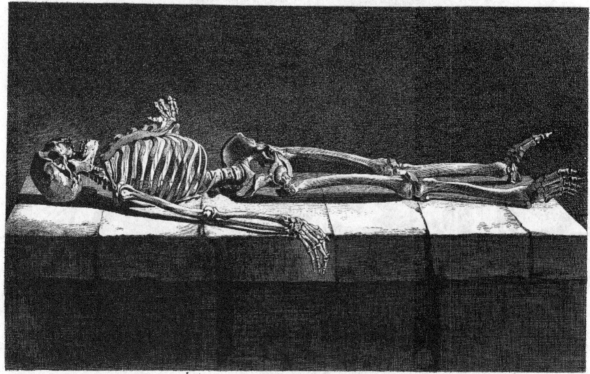

Memento homo quia pulvis es et in pulverem reverteris

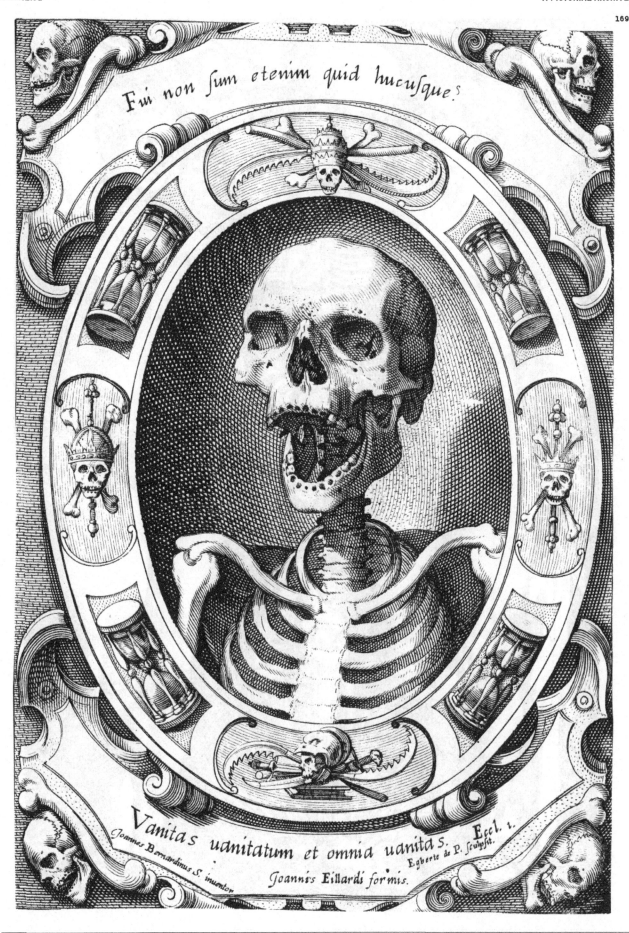

170

172

Vanitas.

Mors ultima linea rerum est. Horat.

P. Schenk fec: et exc: Amstelod:

cum Privil: Ord: Holl: et West Frisiæ.

Hæ sunt primitiæ mortis. Gallus, i eleg.

P. Schenck fec. et exc Amst.   cum Privitt. Ord. Holl. et West Fri.

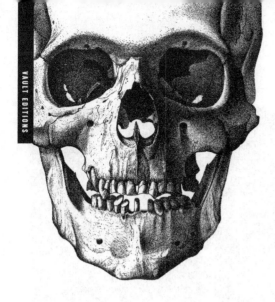

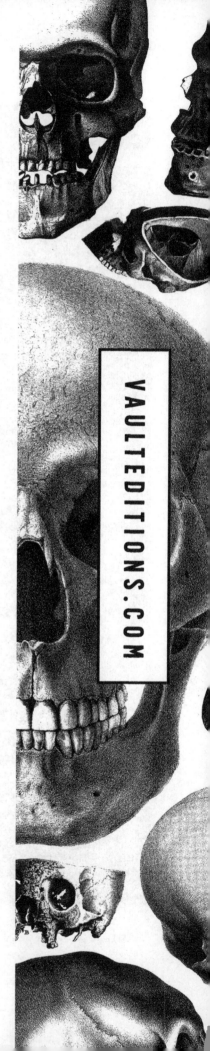

LEARN MORE

At Vault Editions, our mission is to create the world's most diverse and comprehensive collection of image archives available for artists, designers and curious minds. If you have enjoyed this book, you can find more of our titles available at vaulteditions.com.

REVIEW THIS BOOK

As a small, family-owned independent publisher, reviews help spread the word about our work. We would be incredibly grateful if you could leave an honest review of this title wherever you purchased this book.

JOIN OUR COMMUNITY

Are you a creative and curious individual? If so, you will love our community on Instagram. Every day we share bizarre and beautiful artwork ranging from 17th and 18th-century natural history and scientific illustration, to mythical beasts, ornamental designs, anatomical illustration and more. Join our community of 100K+ people today— search @vault_editions on Instagram.

DOWNLOAD YOUR FILES

STEP ONE

Enter the following web address in your web browser on a desktop computer.

www.vaulteditions.com/sas

STEP TWO

Enter the following unique password to access the download page.

s a s 3 8 4 7 2 f s d r x 2

STEP THREE

Follow the prompts to access your high-resolution files.

TECHNICAL ASSISTANCE

For all technical assistance, please email: info@vaulteditions.com

Made in the USA
Las Vegas, NV
04 December 2024

13255396R00059